"*The Holy in the Night* is a profound Advent devotio[n] find safe space for lament, and breathe deeply as we very breath. As a Black woman theologian, Shann[on] her own lived experiences as a spiritual director, p[astor] educator, reclaiming her divinity and freedom. This book not only draws from the biblical narrative but also amplifies the voices of contemporary prophets like Zora Neale Hurston, Audre Lorde, and Cherríe Moraga, recognizing their contributions as carriers of God's still-speaking voice. Using passages from both the Old and New Testaments—many of them challenging ones— as well as modern texts, Dycus invites readers to engage with the complexities of faith while centering the sacred voices that reside in darkness."

— **TERENCE LESTER**, founder of Love Beyond Walls and author of *All God's Children*

"Reading Shannon Dycus's Advent devotional is like watching a gardener describe the warm texture of soil from which faith is born. Through poems, narratives, familiar biblical stories, and wise companions, Dycus draws the reader into a season of the church life that is both longing and freedom. Her reflections break through our layers of everyday exhaustion and lead us to look, listen, and wonder: What is God doing now?"

— **MELISSA FLORER-BIXLER**, author of *How to Have an Enemy* and lead pastor of Raleigh Mennonite Church

"This is a book for all of us who long for a better future while slogging through the world as it is, trudging along with our lives as they are. Shannon Dycus invites us into a posture of patience, of prayer—to notice our breath and wait for God. Because to be where we are is to dwell in the presence of God."

— **ISAAC VILLEGAS**, ordained minister and contributing editor to *Christian Century*

"*The Holy in the Night* offers a grace-filled invitation to dwell in holy darkness during a sometimes too-bright season; it offers a challenging reminder of our freedom in Christ just when we may feel most confined by expectations. Dycus's reflections, sermonettes, and poetic prayers can help us move through

the Advent and Christmas season with renewed attention to the One we anticipate and celebrate."
— **JOANNA HARADER**, author of *Expecting Emmanuel* and pastor of Peace Mennonite Church in Lawrence, Kansas

"In using a staple of many a Christmas playlist to reframe and renew the season of Advent, Shannon W. Dycus is offering us some profound insights. The first one that grabbed my attention and wouldn't let go: 'Marketing and capitalism say go extravagant; Advent says there is value in simple gifts. Advent is resistance.' Alongside such bold claims, Dycus also gently shows us how to interpret our context in harmony with the ancient context that gifted us with our scriptures as well as with a nineteenth-century vision of abolition and emancipation that she invites us to make our own today."
— **MALINDA ELIZABETH BERRY**, associate professor of theology and ethics and director of Faith Formation Collaborative at Anabaptist Mennonite Biblical Seminary

"*The Holy in the Night* fills the much-needed void for Advent devotionals that elevate Black and Brown voices. It is useful for personal and congregational use as we all learn to wait. Shannon Dycus's devotional leads us to wait for Christmas, as we all wait in our current Advent, for our incarnate Lord to come again."
— **JONNY RASHID**, author of *Jesus Takes a Side* and pastor of West Philadelphia Mennonite Church

"Shannon Dycus guides the reader with a beautiful combination of pastoral care, keen scholarship, and an eye on the beauty and complexity of the twenty-first century. Dycus assures us that the Advent journey—our movement toward God—welcomes our fears and our hopes, our joys and our sorrows."
— **REGINA SHANDS STOLTZFUS**, professor of peace, justice, and conflict studies at Goshen College and coauthor of *Been in the Struggle*

THE HOLY
IN THE NIGHT

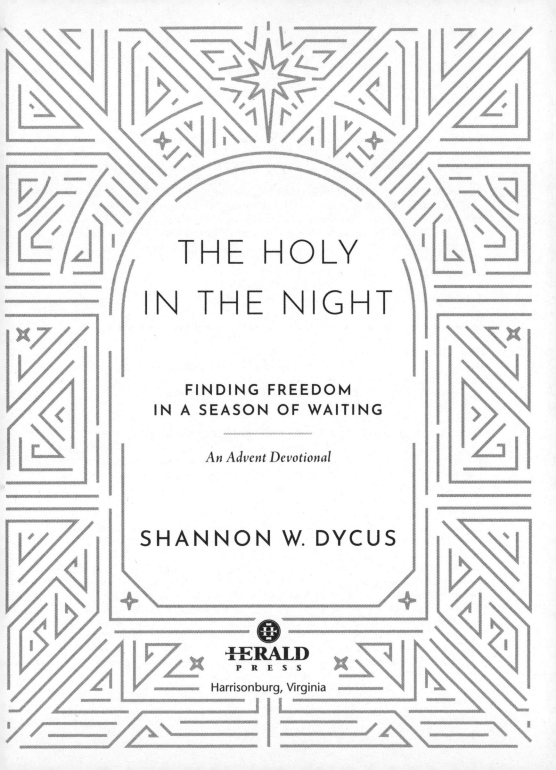

THE HOLY
IN THE NIGHT

FINDING FREEDOM
IN A SEASON OF WAITING

An Advent Devotional

SHANNON W. DYCUS

HERALD
PRESS

Harrisonburg, Virginia

Herald Press
PO Box 866, Harrisonburg, Virginia 22803
www.HeraldPress.com

Names: Dycus, Shannon W., author.
Title: The holy in the night : finding freedom in a season of waiting (an advent devotional) /
    Shannon W. Dycus.
Description: Harrisonburg, Virginia : Herald Press, [2023] | Includes bibliographical
    references.
Identifiers: LCCN 2023022511 (print) | LCCN 2023022512 (ebook) |
    ISBN 9781513813202 (paperback) | ISBN 9781513813219 (ebook)
Subjects: LCSH: Advent. | Devotional calendar. | Devotional literature. |
    BISAC: RELIGION / Christian Living / Devotional | RELIGION / Christian Living /
    Spiritual Growth
Classification: LCC BV40 .D93 2023 (print) | LCC BV40 (ebook) |
    DDC 242/.332—dc23/eng/20230717
LC record available at https://lccn.loc.gov/2023022511
LC ebook record available at https://lccn.loc.gov/2023022512

Study guides are available for many Herald Press titles at www.HeraldPress.com.

THE HOLY IN THE NIGHT
© 2023 by Herald Press, Harrisonburg, Virginia 22803. 800-245-7894. All rights reserved.
Library of Congress Control Number: 2023022511
International Standard Book Number: 978-1-5138-1320-2 (paperback);
    978-1-5138-1321-9 (ebook)
Printed in United States of America
Cover and interior design by Merrill Miller. Cover art adapted from Getty Images.

Unless otherwise noted, Scripture text is taken from the *New Revised Standard Version*
Updated Edition. Copyright © 2021 National Council of Churches of Christ in the United
States of America. Used by permission. All rights reserved worldwide. Scripture quotations
marked (The Inclusive Bible) copyright © 2007 by Priests for Equality, The Inclusive Hebrew
Scriptures, *Volume I: The Torah* (2005), *Volume II: The Prophets* (2004), and *Volume III: The
Writings* (2004). From a Sheed & Ward book, Rowman & Littlefield Publishers, Inc., and pre-
viously published by AltaMira Press. Used by permission. All rights reserved. Scripture quotations marked (NJB) from *The New Jerusalem Bible*, copyright © 1985 by Darton, Longman
& Todd Ltd and *Les Editions du Cerf*, and used by permission of the publishers. Scripture
quotations marked (NKJV) taken from the New King James Version®. Copyright © 1982
by Thomas Nelson, Inc. Used by permission. All rights reserved. Scripture quotations marked
(NLT) are taken from the *Holy Bible*, *New Living Translation*, copyright © 1996, 2004, 2015
by Tyndale House Foundation. Used by permission of Tyndale House Publishers, Inc., Carol
Stream, Illinois 60188. All rights reserved.

27 26 25 24 23   10 9 8 7 6 5 4 3 2 1

To my mother and aunties, who faithfully sat at the Saturday night card tables of singing and laughing, holding holy in your burdened bodies. Seeing God in you has always been my holy place.

CONTENTS

INTRODUCTION

We spend much of our lives in waiting rooms, literal and metaphorical —those difficult, sacred, in-between spaces of life where we don't know the outcome. So many of our days are anticipatory, held in short waiting periods until the other side of meetings, test results, that next birthday. These are often layered on top of longer seasons of waiting—*as soon as a relationship feels stable, once I finish school, when we have enough money, after the kids grow up, as soon as the world calms the heck down.*

Instead of allowing us to hold space for these unknowns, many of our cultures have taught us to expect—have in fact demanded—that we produce specific, measurable results. To respond with "I don't know" or to sit with what is most true rather than push past it toward an immediate resolution is considered irresponsible. We are shamed for feeling the natural anxiety that accompanies such uncertainty and lack permission to say, "I am not okay yet." Instead, we perform "okayness" for ourselves and for one another. We become incapable of waiting well.

To compound our impatience, we categorize experiences of waiting, unknowing, confusion as seasons of darkness. Anytime *we* cannot see and control our spheres, we name it dark and separate it from the reach of God.

But the winter tree hangs naked for months.

And pregnant bellies protrude gradually.

And the magi traveled for months following the star to find Jesus.

That time was not wasted. Between daylights, Divine work endures. What if we're free enough to do the same?

In a spiritual reflection on Holy Saturday, the quiet period in between Jesus' death and resurrection, priest and author Barbara Brown Taylor offers this truth: "Between the great dramas of life, there is almost always a time of empty waiting—with nothing to do and no church service to help—a time when it is necessary to come up with your own words and see how they sound with no other sounds to cover them up."[1]

In these spaces in between, there is room for us to engage the work of God. Even as these empty in-between spaces call us to wait, the invitation to be present persists. The spaces in between daylight nudge at our spirits in different and important ways. The season of Advent captures the essence of this invitation from the empty in-between.

What if we trusted God enough to show up in between blessings?

What if we understood that we could be both anxious and faithful? What if we were able to recognize the presence of fear and God at the same time?

What if we reframed our sense of waiting periods to notice divine presence?

What if hope could be less about outcomes and more about peace in our unknowing?

In Advent we find ways to keep listening for God when we don't know the answers to our questions. This liturgical season when we await the promised birth of our Savior holds deep resonance for our desires to be faithful in waiting. Advent embodies unknowing and uncertainty—with permission—and the legitimate and faithful congruence of waiting and faithfulness. We journey with Mary and Joseph through the patience and trust that pregnancy requires. We journey with the magi through the anguish of their deep need for God to do a new thing in the world.

In this devotional, my hope is to stretch open our possibilities for faithfulness during silence, darkness, ambivalence, doubt, and unknowing. I write as a spiritual director and pastor, as a mother and spouse, and as an educator committed to listening and learning in community. I write this as a Black girl reclaiming my divinity and freedom. I write this from the Shenandoah Valley of the United States, where sitting low accentuates the wonder of God. These labels feel like repetitions of the ways I have witnessed and known the presence of God in grace, struggle, and beauty. Advent incarnates the language and longings that feel most real between God and me. Without expertise or certitude, I stand with your spirit, and point toward a God whom I trust will continue to be made known.

From Advent to Epiphany, this book offers an invitation for each day. Most of them are written from the biblical narrative in which this season is rooted. Some of them are written from contemporary prophets, whom I believe carry the still-speaking voice of God. Each invitation gives us space to see again the ways that God has invited us into new ways of thinking and being, that we might inhabit seasons of waiting differently.

I believe that God uses Advent to call us beyond the language, the fears, and traditions that limit our ability to anticipate the sacred. My prayer is that we hold new invitations with boldness and grace, that we might be freed to receive God anew.

USING THIS DEVOTIONAL

The thirty-six daily devotions in this book are undated and can be used in any year. They are divided into six themes, generally following the six weeks of Advent, Christmas, and Epiphany. While the earliest possible start date for Advent is November 27, you may wish to begin on December 1 to align the days of the month with the divisions included here. The Small Group Guide starting on page 139 offers additional reflections for gathering with others, or can be used for further personal contemplation and prayer throughout the season.

The daily reflections revolve around three rhythms: listening, reflections on freedom, and breath prayers.

Listen

Intentionally, I refrain from the word *read*. While reading is included, consider the deeper digesting of taking in the words as you experience them logically and emotionally, with curiosity and critique. The scriptures in this devotional are from the Revised Common Lectionary, a resource used across many Western Christian churches that presents three-year cycles of the Bible. Like a daily lesson, the lectionary offers a set of scriptures for each Sunday or Christian holy day. Within each set of reflections, I include passages from all three years and across the Old and New Testaments. Some of these scriptures are complicated and difficult. As you identify your comfort with them, welcome what is true for you into your listening.

Some of the readings are from modern texts written by prophets of our time. From voices and experiences that affirm that God's Spirit has remained among us, my canon extends beyond the biblical Scriptures, and I highlight Black and Brown voices to remind us of the sacred voice that lives in darkness.

The final day in each set of reflections includes fragments of sermons connected to the theme that draw on biblical texts that are not part of the Advent scriptures. These are invitations to hear God's word beyond this season as we are making habits to carry it forward. The sermon reflections in the Small Group Guide starting on page 139 expand on these sermonettes.

Freedom

In its simplest form, being free means having the space or power to make choices that reflect the truth of our lives. For example, when you trust a friend enough to admit your loneliness to them, you experience freedom. Our relationships with God inspire honest and faithful choices, and our spiritual lives help us sustain habits that ground us in those God-inspired choices. These choices are muddied by our own self-doubts, the scarcities and fears of others, and significant systemic forces. Seasons like Advent and Lent are designed for us to intentionally access the truths we are holding and a nearness to God. Choosing and choosing truth is not easy or even natural. It requires that we unpack some of the logic and practices we carry to clarify who chose it and who benefits.

Many of the daily invitations introduce the line "I am free to" as a reminder that there is permission for us to think, believe, do, and choose differently as acts of faith. The invitations start in freedom to give ourselves space to tell new truths.

Breath prayers

Most of the daily invitations conclude with a breath prayer. They are intended to help you remember the concepts of the invitation and to welcome the wisdom you need into your body and your rhythm. Breath prayers are a gift from desert mothers and fathers who taught that connecting our prayers with our breath enhances our mindfulness. Breathing is our constant connection to the foundation of our humanity and our spirituality as we consider God's initial breath into living bodies.

I often return to breath prayers during my day, setting the words of the prayer as an alarm on my phone or an event on my calendar. Feel free to incorporate breath prayers in ways that make sense for you. Give yourself permission to do full inhalations and exhalations, breathing in through your nose and out through your mouth. This reconnects your physical body with your spiritual and mental intentions.

Behold, the glistening sign of hope.

A distant but shining star is
cupped by the darkness
that holds gently
our future.

Do we dare to feel its warming glow
in these days so cold with fear?

Do we dare to wonder where it leads us,
or choose the path we know?

The Holy has painted possibility
across the night sky.

It flickers with potential,
trembles with vulnerability,
shimmers with beauty, still.

Come, seekers.

The journey is before us.
A new day is born.[2]
          —M Jade Kaiser

AN INVITATION TO THE SONG

O holy night! The stars are brightly shining;
it is the night of our dear Savior's birth.
Long lay the world in sin and error pining,
till he appeared and the soul felt its worth.
A thrill of hope, the weary world rejoices,
for yonder breaks a new and glorious morn!
Fall on your knees; O hear the angel voices!
O night divine, O night when Christ was born!
O night, O holy night, O night divine!
—Placide Cappeau de Roquemaure, "O Holy Night"

After you read the lyrics from "O Holy Night," I encourage you to listen to the song once or twice. Artists Jennifer Hudson and Martina McBride have beautiful renditions. For a worshipful version with all the verses, listen to gospel singer Kim Burrell.

"O Holy Night," written in 1847, is one of the most popular Christmas songs in North American contexts and beyond. The song began as a French poem by Cappeau then set to music by a Jewish classical musician popular in Catholic masses until their faith practices were questioned. Still, across time and genre, many Christian communities approach this song in their celebrations holding the narrative and hope of Christ's coming. The song tells a story centered on the scene of this birth in the night and an even darker backdrop of our world.

The lyrics of the song give us permission to pay specific attention to the starry night and distant angelic sounds. Playing on our concepts of the dark, the song captures the mystery and tranquility with a melody that maintains a simple and repetitive scale. We get drawn into an uncomplicated rhythm as the vocals build to introduce the holy and majestic.

A thrill of hope, the weary world rejoices.

These words hold the essence and the tension of the Christmas narrative. The world into which Jesus came was weary. Weary of Roman occupation. Weary of religious oppression. Weary of waiting for the promise of the Messiah to be fulfilled. Many of us can relate to this weariness, if not from the stresses of the holidays, then within our personal situations. And yet some aspect of the holidays is a reminder of something comforting and peaceful, something that reintroduces a bit of hope and rejoicing.

Faaaaalllll on your knees.
O hhhheeeaaarrr the angel voices!

In every version, this crescendo and lyrics capture me as the note is sustained and strong. In this night, we are summoned to settle and listen—for there is divine work before us. In many of our Christmas songs, we rush to the light of the morning and the beautiful swaddling of a baby. "O Holy Night" affirms that this night is holy. While there is sweat and blood, fatigue and awe, the forming of a brand-new family, this night is holy; this night is divine.

This song finds us before Christmas breaks in with all its lights and splendor. It catches us before the upbeat melodies and the moment when "all is bright." This song portrays the messy night before all the joy is holy and Love is still swaddled, quiet, and vulnerable. "O Holy Night" asks us to squint through darkness with a small wonder for its unique capacity to bear the divine.

O HOLY NIGHT

The possibility of freedom

The title of this book reframes the familiar Christmas song "O Holy Night," which starts with these three words. This phrase is contradictory. Our notions of the night are often scary and dangerous. The language of darkness that fills the night is aligned with sin and death. We elevate and center our faith on finding the Light. How can the night be holy?

The central themes of Advent embody this contradiction. Our calendars say *go*; Advent says *slow down*. Hasty Christmas music and social obligations maintain a constant volume; Advent says *find silence*. Marketing and capitalism say *go extravagant*; Advent says *there is value in simple gifts*. Advent is resistance. It is a season to recalibrate our spirits by accepting the invitations to slow down, find silence, and seek the simple.

"O Holy Night" introduces a possibility, one that showcases the Advent message. Resistant to the norms and the powers that fuel the norms, "O Holy Night" suggests that something new might be possible. The season makes a space for us to draw closer to ourselves and God, finding freedoms we haven't known before.

There is possibility of peace in this season.

There is possibility of wisdom in this in-between.

There is possibility of holy in the night.

DAY 1

Listen

It is so easy to be hopeful in the daytime when you can see the things you wish on. But it was night, it stayed night. Night was striding across nothingness with the whole round world in [God's] hands. . . . They sat in company with the others in other shanties, their eyes straining against cruel walls and their souls asking if [God] meant to measure their puny might against [God's]. They seemed to be staring at the dark, but their eyes were watching God.[3]

—**Zora Neale Hurston**, *Their Eyes Were Watching God*

i am free to unlearn.

In the biblical narratives of creation, God began in the dark. In soil, wombs, and resurrection morning, God duplicates the darkness as a marker of beginning. Like a studio space, there is creative power in God's darkness.

Yet pervasive in our Advent theology and practices is a desire to dismiss and overcome the darkness as if it presents a threat to our humanity or our faithfulness. That we are displaced in moments or seasons of darkness is a myth. Light is not a correction to darkness, and they do not exist as binaries in competition for our desire. Just as sunsets display a colorful dance, what if we held them as we see them and let light and darkness be in relationship with one another?

Yet we've let ourselves live in fear and opposition to the dark, fighting to limit its presence in our lives. We associate it with loneliness and godlessness, separated from our growth and well-being. The Advent myth of darkness steals the possibilities of what we can learn from this season. Just as light illuminates, there are ways of being learned only in the dark. Dark nights and seasons without light are legitimate and sacred spaces of learning.

Writer and anthropologist Zora Neale Hurston believed in the gift of darkness, as it enriched her spirituality and her identity. Finding God in the darkness of the night and in her skin became a way to imagine and dream with the Divine. Hurston's genius in *Their Eyes Were Watching God* gives us the chance to actively unlearn the myths of darkness with our own practices. "They seemed to be staring at the dark, but their eyes were watching God." To look into a starry night and see God helps us reform the relationship of darkness and the Divine in our minds and our spirits. What if we looked into a dark night and experienced the presence of God just as when we gaze at well-lit pulpits?

The myth of darkness perpetuates our perceived control and comfort in the presence of light. We assume clarity and awareness, maintaining resistance to mystery and unknowing. Writer and artist Morgan Harper Nichols says, "There is a reason the sky gets dark at night—we were not meant to see everything all the time. We were meant to trust even in the darkness."[4]

Advent is a season to learn the sounds and rhythm of the darkness. It is intended to strengthen our faith in seasons when we cannot depend on vision and light. We are invited to unlearn our inclinations to perceive darkness and unknowing as a deficiency and to welcome Advent as a season that dances with the seasons of our life.

What if we committed to watching God when we feel waves of nothingness, cruelty, or puniness? What if we freed our expectations to see God in the night?

Breath prayer

Inhale: I can see new life,

Exhale: even in the dark.

DAY 2

Listen

I was glad when they said to me,
  "Let us go to the house of the LORD!"
Our feet are standing
  within your gates, O Jerusalem.
  —Psalm 122:1-2

i am free to breathe deeply.

In the old-school African American church that I grew up in, these words of the psalmist began many a worship service. When I read these lines, they still have the tone of the old deacons who announced this phrase with confidence across a squeaky PA system. This declaration was the sounding call that worship was beginning and God was going to meet us.

Psalm 122 is located within the section of Psalms called Songs of Ascent, which celebrate the ways we choose to move toward God. Specifically, this psalm names the temple of Jerusalem, and what was assumed to be a pilgrimage to this holy place. The remainder of the psalm expands on the significance of Jerusalem and the blessings that have been brought because of its steadiness as a gathering place for many tribes with leaders who follow God.

If we were hearing this passage in the Hebrew context, we would also be attuned to the unnamed idiom that "going to Jerusalem" also meant going "up" because the city of Jerusalem sits at the top of a mountain about twenty-five hundred feet above sea level. The pilgrimage includes both a literal and a symbolic ascent, the work of going higher to seek God.

Let's talk about ascending. What happens as we climb?

At whatever altitude we find ourselves, there is always an ocean of air above us. As we ascend, the air becomes thinner because there are fewer molecules in it. Most importantly, higher altitudes of air contain less oxygen. Our bodies are amazing, and they know how to adapt. We begin to breathe faster and more deeply to ensure that oxygen continues to flow through our blood and through to our brain and muscles. This happens as we climb, sing, exercise, or perform other activities where our access or need for fresh air changes. We are technically hyperventilating—but in a way that our body can understand and process so that our lung functioning and health actually improve over time.

Breathing consistently at high altitudes does something slightly different to our lungs. Our lungs begin to expand, increasing capacity for the continuous ventilation that occurs with less oxygen. Can you imagine the literal impact on the bodies of those who made this journey regularly? Between the singing and the climbing, the psalmists knew that one of the impacts of being in Jerusalem was beginning to breathe differently.

"Let us go to the house of the LORD!" becomes a richer invitation. And I think those old deacons somehow knew all this. It is not only a pilgrimage to a holy and beloved place where we encounter God. It is also an invitation to journey into what is changing in our atmosphere and into how we might be open to new patterns of living and breathing.

In this new season of Advent, may we ascend to the gates of Jerusalem. Not in ways that seek more power or productivity but in ways of being that welcome intimate time with God where we walk at a pace with attention to our breath.

Breath prayer

Inhale: **God is within me.**

Exhale: **And we journey together.**

Listen

But about that day and hour no one knows, neither the angels of heaven, nor the Son, but only the Father. For as the days of Noah were, so will be the coming of the Son of Man. For as in the days before the flood they were eating and drinking, marrying and giving in marriage, until the day Noah entered the ark, and they knew nothing until the flood came and swept them all away, so, too, will be the coming of the Son of Man.

—Matthew 24:36–39

i am free to . . . not know.

The scriptures of Advent begin with a song of gladness from the Psalms and an invitation into God's presence from the prophet Isaiah and these . . . stressful . . . words from the gospel of Matthew.

In Matthew 24, we read the direct but ambiguous words of Jesus, where he names our inability to anticipate what God is about to do—connecting it back to the story of Noah and the flood, particularly to the ignorance of those alive just before that catastrophic event swept them off the face of the earth. For Christians who have tried to be faithful, hearing "No one knows" is tragic. We go to church, are prayerful, and sing melodies so that we can know the mind of God and be attuned to the moves of God. In our fear, this passage might inspire in us a sense of hurried need: a need to be prepared and to figure out what we don't yet know.

And yet verse 36 assures, "No one knows"—neither the angels nor the Son. Contrary to what we might have expected, Jesus is not preaching a sermon of preparedness. It's not that we're simply out of the loop and must work to restore missing information or resources. There is no loop. There is no way to know. What we read in this passage is a homily of uncertainty.

In the flood narrative of Genesis 6–7, Noah experienced his own in-between period, not knowing or hearing from God. Initially, God offered guidance to Noah on how to prepare the ark and direction to enter it with his family and the animals. But in the climax of the story, when Noah and his family actually lived on the ark, God's guidance and direction seem nowhere to be found. It rained for forty days straight, with waters seemingly ready to overcome the boat and all who took shelter on it. They remained on the ark for almost a year.

In the absence of God's voice or direction, Noah became attentive. The Scriptures say he "opened the window of the ark" (Genesis 8:6). Using the birds and their responsiveness, Noah commenced a rhythm of sending and waiting and learning until a dove confirmed that the waters had subsided.

Similarly, in our times of unknowing, we awaken to the possibility to actively notice God working around us. This passage in Matthew closes with the instruction to keep a watchful eye. It's as if God is dialed in to how reliant we are on our logic and our need to control by being hyper-prepared. Speaking from and to the Judaic tradition, Jesus and Matthew refer to the well-known story of Noah, using collective memory to strengthen faithfulness when life feels out of our control and God feels silent. They knew Noah's story would remind the people that God has done this before—been silent but instructive, pointing us where to look. What initially feels like stress is a narrative reminder of how to make our way through Advent: open the window and listen.

The scriptures of Advent begin with this message of uncertainty, providing an intentional way for us to navigate this season of being "in between." While we can acknowledge all the ways that not knowing can be frightening, the invitation of this passage and for you this Advent is to remember that God knows. We now step into a whole season that nudges us into a faithfulness that restores our trust in God's wisdom.

God knew for Noah. And God knows for you in this stressful in-between season. God will know for what is to come. We don't have to.

Breath prayer

Inhale: I don't have to know.

Exhale: The wisdom of God is enough.

DAY 4

Listen

Yet you are our mother and father, YHWH;
we are the clay and you are the potter,
we are all the work of your hands.

—Isaiah 64:8 (The Inclusive Bible)

a prayer for new edges

you are the potter, where are you?
i am the clay, thrown by all the winds around me

you are the potter, with hands that become peaceful harbor
i am the clay, ease my weighted breath

you are the potter, set hope in the dust of the stars
i am the clay, keep me from the lie of my undeserving

you are the potter, may your gaze remind and remember
i am the clay, mold me slowly into my already

you are the potter, shape me free

DAY 5

Listen

"There will be signs in the sun, the moon, and the stars and on the earth distress among nations confused by the roaring of the sea and the waves. People will faint from fear and foreboding of what is coming upon the world, for the powers of the heavens will be shaken. Then they will see 'the Son of Man coming in a cloud' with power and great glory. Now when these things begin to take place, stand up and raise your heads, because your redemption is drawing near."

Then he told them a parable: "Look at the fig tree and all the trees; as soon as they sprout leaves you can see for yourselves and know that summer is already near. So also, when you see these things taking place, you know that the kingdom of God is near. Truly I tell you, this generation will not pass away until all things have taken place. Heaven and earth will pass away, but my words will not pass away."

–Luke 21:25-33

i am free to have many parts.

This passage from Luke 21 includes all the standard apocalyptic drama—creation is disturbed, the "Son of Man" is present and powerful, and the revelation is drawing near. Scriptures like this remind the reader in a literal and theological sense that the end of the world is looming, and it will happen with catastrophe and destruction. This is no baby in swaddling clothes. This is not Christmas. While we anticipate the beauty of new birth, we will address the possibility of tragedy. Beyond all the lights and garlands perfectly perched around us, the conversation of Advent is honest and visceral.

In this first week of Advent, these reflections highlight several passages that include petition and praise to God, but most of them focus on the coming of Christ in the apocalyptic sense. Scripture leans toward the telling of end times, Christ's return, and how the reign concludes. More importantly, there is no cute passage about Mary or Joseph and their pending gift. (Spoiler alert: We don't get there until just before Christmas.) Advent is not fully about Christmas. It's a season connected to the events and themes of Christmas, but there is more. Advent is the season within which Christmas lives; it holds the ways we prepare for the moves of God in and around Christmas.

The tone of Advent is intentional. It seeks to tell a complete story of hope and fear, beginning and ending, distressed seas and sprouting fig trees. And it gives us permission to tell complete stories. These next few weeks bring pockets of joy, but they also remind us of the grief we carry. We see opportunities for continual giving, and we are aware of our own financial limitations. Babies and births and beginnings are not comfortable places for all of us. The parts of us that hold this discomfort are indeed parts of the complete story of Advent that we are being drawn into.

This passage of Luke is a prophetic wake-up call. We are asked to name our loneliness and how easily we lean into performing parts of ourselves that aren't true. We are asked to admit our sense of abandonment from God and our deep hunger for divine presence. The honest, fragile, falling-apart pieces of ourselves are included in the whole story of Advent. It is with this story that we experience the nearness of God. Hope begins with a recognition of what is, not what it should be or is intended to be. Then, from our current state of brokenness, we anticipate a coming.

The fig tree is a frequent biblical image, related to how Israel is connected and healthy with God. What's highlighted in a fig tree is that its fruit buds before the leaves. The leaves of a fig tree are steady remains after the edible fruit. With attention to a fig tree's varied parts, we are guided to the presence of leaves on the fig tree as a sign of steadiness. Luke's words are a sign that the seasons are continuous, the earth is flourishing, and the figs have already come from the tree. The story continues as we notice its different parts. The fig and its leaf, the fruit and its covering, our truth and its buffer—together, these tell of God's coming.

Breath prayer

Inhale: I can start with what is;

Exhale: **God becomes closer as I start.**

DAY 6

Listen

Then Job arose, tore his robe, shaved his head, and fell on the ground and worshiped. He said, "Naked I came from my mother's womb, and naked shall I return there; the Lord gave, and the Lord has taken away; blessed be the name of the Lord."

In all this Job did not sin or charge God with wrongdoing. . . .

So the accuser went out from the presence of the Lord and inflicted loathsome sores on Job from the sole of his foot to the crown of his head. Job took a potsherd with which to scrape himself and sat among the ashes.

Then his wife said to him, "Do you still persist in your integrity? Curse God and die." But he said to her, "You speak as any foolish woman would speak. Shall we receive good from God and not receive evil?" In all this Job did not sin with his lips.

–Job 1:20-22; 2:7-10

SERMONETTE

Job and Job's Wife: Making Sense of Darkness

One of my lenses in reading the Bible is to listen for the women. Realistically, the Bible was written and transmitted in a male-centric way, and to hear the women requires intentionality. As a woman who lives with and seeks to proclaim what the Bible points to, one way to hear the women of the Bible is to look for how I find myself in these stories. As I listen for the women in the book of Job, I wonder about Job's wife.

Job's wife appears in only two small portions of the forty-two chapters. She is referenced in Job 19:17, when Job responds to his friends, reminding them of his losses and social isolation. We hear her speak only once in chapter 2, which we highlight in this study. In verse 9, she says, "Do you still persist in your integrity? Curse God and die." To name what is obvious but is not stated, Job's wife also has endured significant loss. She has also lost her children, her home, her stability, and their legacy. It's likely she has been a witness to the grief of Job while carrying her own. She, too, is inviting the question of faithfulness and suffering.

Job's wife is not a character we know much about. Her context is nebulous. We also technically do not know whether Job and his family are Jewish, nor do we know the happenings in their homeland of Uz, which was an Edomite or Aramean territory. Moreover, we do not know the lens of who is writing, since the writer, or writers, as most scholars think, is also unknown. In short, more is unknown than known.

A resource that becomes helpful as we listen to the stories of women is the Jewish practice of midrash. Midrash is a type of biblical interpretation that invites rabbis to share underlying significance in non-legal portions of scripture. The Jewish Women's Archive, an online archive that documents both ancient and modern stories of Jewish women, shares several midrashic interpretations of Job's wife that include negative and positive perspectives on her role and intention.

In an article from this archive, we hear a common correlation, though surprising for most Christians, made between Job's wife and Eve. The role and impact of Eve in the creation narratives become a parallel for viewing Job's partner.

In the view of the midrash, [Job's wife] acted in a fashion similar to Eve, who encouraged Adam to sin. Job, however, learned from the precedent of Adam, and did not heed his wife. He said: I am not like Adam. He listened to his wife, and sinned by eating of the Tree of

Knowledge. But I did not heed my wife, I did not curse the Lord, and I did not sin.[5]

Listeners to the Job narrative might initially hear the strength and power of Job's wife and be reminded of how Eve was also strong and powerful in how she influenced Adam. And in this interpretation, just as Eve's efforts were sinful, so must be the efforts of Job's wife. This parallel has unnecessarily marginalized the voice of Job's wife (and Eve), requiring that we assume a negative connotation in her words. Because we have marginalized her, we have separated her from the healing that Job ultimately receives in this narrative. Instead of combining the stories of Eve and Job's wife into one, and therefore conflating the impact of female voice in the scriptures, I'd like to pay attention to the particular invitation of her words.

A voice of doubt

Job's wife begins with a question: "Do you still persist in your integrity?" Made early in the book, this question is in fresh response to their losses. Job's wife is present to the integrity and commitment of Job during these trials and opens a space where he might question his desire or capacity to endure. For centuries, we have interpreted this statement as one that demeans Job's loyalty and questions his relationship to God. Hers is a voice of doubt. She introduces the possibility of not continuing as he has. She asks this hard question. But what if we resist the urge to categorize her question as an assault to his faith?

Another way to hear her question would be, "Are you going to make it if you continue like this?" If we look for how we find ourselves in this story, as I suggested earlier, we may realize that we actually ask questions like this all the time. Consider times when we see a friend or family member about to embark on something large and intimidating and ask, "Are you going to make it?" Or think about that friend who's headed for another date with that guy she was doubting after the first text. Our entire intention is not to question whether the task can be completed, but to ask whether this is the right and best choice.

When moving toward a grand act, sometimes the worst scenario is to almost make it. So we sometimes question for the sake of care. And let's be real, we sometimes offer questions as a sanity check.

Job's wife follows this question with a weighty suggestion: "Curse God and die." These words have often echoed as reasoning to discount her voice and nullify her support of her husband in their trials. Her suggestions to curse and die are the extreme opposite of a faithful response, yet she vocalizes them. Again, our traditional response to her words is negative and assumptive. I'd like to suspend those and empathize with her position.

An honest faith

While Job's desire for health and wholeness is enacted through a righteous faithfulness, his wife's is offered in authenticity. While he firmly moves toward God, she attempts to deconstruct their reality as a path to understanding. "Curse God and die" is a harsh, startling statement. It conveys her capacity to be present to their tragedies as it reveals a depth of emotion we do not sense from Job. In this statement, Job's wife is human and complex—actively wrestling with a God who deals in such suffering, reminiscent of Jacob. Her form of faith is honest and authentic, outwardly revealing her deepest fears.

I have been where she is. When things are bad, there is little hope, and I say to myself, "Okay, what is the very worst that could happen?" In one instance I had been traveling for work and left my sick husband at home with our two young children. I tried calling his phone to check on him, with no responses. My brain immediately started producing worst-case scenarios: He's unconscious, my kids are terrified, his phone is dead, the doors are locked . . . and on and on. I let my brain wander into my very deepest fears to produce the worst outcomes to the situation. He called, wearily, as I wandered through these terrors, and he told me all was well. In the psychology world, this mental practice is called defensive pessimism. It is often used to manage anxiety: individuals prepare themselves mentally for a poor outcome and can be more resilient in the face of that actuality.

Just as we process through the worst possibilities in moments of fear, maybe Job's wife was doing the same. Perhaps she did not offer "Curse God, and die" as a literal suggestion, but for the sake of their shared resilience, named the very worst thing that could happen to them in that moment. Without the benefit of our lofty words and modern psychology, she somehow knew she could name this ridiculous possibility to propel them in the opposite direction. Maybe her doubt and authenticity opened a space that led to the endurance they needed to move through their suffering.

The book of Job is hard. It raises more questions than it answers. *How can I understand my doubts as blessings? When can my uncertainty lead to resilience?* Maybe the answers are to find expressions of our faith in the questions, trusting that the questions themselves strengthen our relationship with God. And as we ask our questions, may we know healing in believing that we can come as imperfectly as we are into God's presence. Amen.

THE STARS ARE BRIGHTLY SHINING

Tools for the night

Advent is an experience of the night—moving toward God through our own realities of chaos and pain without fully knowing how things continue or end. "O Holy Night" reminds us that we are given guidance for traversing the night in tools like stars.

Depending on where you are, stars can offer varying infusions of light for the ways ahead. Stars in the night of the countryside are less muted by the impacts of our lives and are going to be more revelatory than stars in the city sky. Still, stars break through in even the most polluted skies.

What we find in the stars is also found in us. Scientists continue to learn about the parallels between the composition of the stars and the human body, revealing that nearly all the elements in the human body were made in a star. Oxygen, hydrogen, potassium, sodium, magnesium, phosphorous, carbon—it goes on. The elements that contribute to the stars offering light in the darkness are the same elements within our bodies—reminding us that the wisdom and Spirit within us are our internal stars and tools for navigating the night. For this Advent, our practices of contemplation and awareness of spirituality are tools for in-between seasons of light. God has prepared us.

DAY 7

Listen

How do I hold faith with sun in a sunless place? It is so hard not to counter this despair with a refusal to see. But I have to stay open and filtering no matter what's coming at me, because that arms me in a particularly Black woman's way. When I'm open, I'm also less despairing. The more clearly I see what I'm up against, the more able I am to fight this process going on in my body that they're calling liver cancer. And I am determined to fight it even when I am not sure of the terms of the battle nor the face of victory. . . .

Living with cancer has forced me to consciously jettison the myth of omnipresence, of believing—or loosely asserting—that I can do anything, along with any dangerous illusion of immortality. Neither of these unscrutinized defenses is a solid base for either political activism or personal struggle. But in their place, another kind of power is growing, tempered and enduring, grounded within the realities of what I am in fact doing. An open-eyed assessment and appreciation of what I can and do accomplish, using who I am and who I most wish myself to be. To stretch as far as I can go and relish what is satisfying rather than what is sad. Building a strong and elegant pathway toward transition.[6]

–**Audre Lorde,** *A Burst of Light and Other Essays*

i am free to turn.

Audre Lorde lived until 1992 as a prophetic poet, activist, and philosopher. In *A Burst of Light*, she compiles a series of essays that chronicle some of her most personal thoughts around life through social, political, and emotional lenses. As a queer woman of color in her contexts, Lorde remained familiar with vulnerability and truth. This book presents her consistent honesty as she looks inward and at her own life.

The first paragraph of today's text is taken from the final chapter of the book and her personal journal entitled "Living with Cancer," where Lorde recounts her first three years journeying with cancer. Much like the journey of Advent, Lorde speaks of sunless places and not knowing the terms or how her battle will conclude. The darkness and unknowing are real and proximate for Lorde, as she asks how to maintain her faith. In her responses, remaining open and committing to see are primary ways she persists in her journey. The reality of her diagnosis means she is waiting for and needing revelation. Instead of specific actions that suggest certainty, Lorde offers the wisdom of posture—openness and seeing: ways to welcome new information in times of unknowing.

In the second paragraph, drawn from the epilogue of the book, Lorde expands on her posture of uncertainty, naming how she understands her power differently. Instead of omnipresence, she names grounded reality and attention to capacity and satisfaction as tools for her new patterns.

Throughout the book, Lorde returns to the imagery of "turning fear into fire," language that seems to reflect how she navigates the courage of her voice and identity and how she was choosing to face cancer and even death. While her grasp of fear and fire are important, they are familiar concepts in the scope of her scholarship. In some of her other work, Lorde discusses approaches to "living inside oneself" with the vulnerability and intimacy that give her knowledge of both fear and fire.

While transitions are very common, what is most moving about this idea of turning fear into fire is the intended transition from one state of being to another. "Turning" is an act of power and courage, exhibiting strength in how one prioritizes what is important. Fear and its ability to control and invite scarcity is disempowered to give space for fire that gives light and warmth and has capacity to ignite more fire. Like the invitation of Epiphany, the movement from fear into fire is an intentional shift from darkness to light. Lorde does this turning by using new postures and relearning her power—choosing to respond differently to her realities and allowing something new to be revealed in her and to her.

Breath prayer

Inhale: What I am holding

Exhale: can shift to be what I need.

DAY 8

Listen

In those days John the Baptist appeared in the wilderness of Judea, proclaiming, "Repent, for the kingdom of heaven has come near." This is the one of whom the prophet Isaiah spoke when he said,

> "The voice of one crying out in the wilderness:
> 'Prepare the way of the Lord;
> make his paths straight.'"

Now John wore clothing of camel's hair with a leather belt around his waist, and his food was locusts and wild honey. Then Jerusalem and all Judea and all the region around the Jordan were going out to him, and they were baptized by him in the River Jordan, confessing their sins.

—Matthew 3:1-6

in the wilderness, i am free.

As we begin this chapter in Matthew, John brings the message of a new kingdom—news that would call for celebration. This is basically a call for a party. The appropriate response is to start getting ready for a feast and worship in the temple.

Except John proclaims a message of repentance. Repent? Go ask for forgiveness for my sins? Right now? Isn't that the point of a new kingdom of heaven—to start over?

We know John the Baptizer as the old-school preacher who is honest and tough as he prepares us for the coming of Jesus. John is judgmental, uncomfortably calling for a sense of responsibility to both the old and the new. For the people of Jerusalem and Judea, his message lands as unpopular and unconventional. Instead of holding a joyful sense of anticipation, he is saying, "Wait, we need to get ourselves right." John is calling for realignment, identifying the coming newness as a chance to recalibrate to the Spirit of God. Instead of expecting the new to come and simply wash away the old, John's message suggests we must hold and own our truth so that it may be transformed.

In the spirit of preparation, John tells the truth. Our transitions into new seasons cannot begin with our expectation that the new simply replaces old—we must reconcile the two.

Yet the most significant detail of John's truth that helps us live into this is not its content; it's his location. John appears in the wilderness. In his cultural context, when you had something important to name or declare, you went to the center of the city, the locus of power. The wilderness is the opposite.

John's prophecy includes his intentional distance from power, an act that resists practice and culture. But this is a difficult way to convey this message. For the people of Israel, memories of the wilderness align with the struggle of John's current message. The revelation of the Torah and the death of a generation in the wilderness hold themes of both judgment and redemption within this location.

By definition, the wilderness is one of the purest settings, holding an ecosystem of living and dying organisms. A wilderness is messy and unkept, allowed to grow in its most natural state without human interruption. Just as we do with the darkness, we often hold the wilderness as a metaphoric location and season of godlessness. We see wilderness in a singular view of loneliness, separating it from its larger opportunities away from people and power and in the flow of growth. But the wilderness is affected by other aspects of nature: trees pruned by the wind, leaves decomposing with the snow, and mammals consuming critters. It's a space where change, the most organic and generative, is held.

When I think about ways to find wilderness in my own life, it often includes getting out of my normal environment and seeking silence. In other times, it includes honest conversations with friends who hold me as a messy and powerful human. The titles of Reverend or Dean are unimportant. To them, I'm Shanny or Dub—an impatient critic of all things somebody else did wrong. But in this wilderness, I am held accountable to my own winds and storms.

Before we can move ahead, we've got to account for the mistakes we've made. So let's step away from the places where we feel important to let ourselves be shaped by the natural forces of change. This is hard work that John is prompting.

In our own relationships with truth and truth telling, we can look to John, who models the place from where we can stand in the most truth for seasons of preparation. John does not speak from the center, where people and power do the shaping. His truth helps us see that we must ground our truth telling in raw and simple places. They, too, are sacred.

Breath prayer

Inhale: I can step away from the center,

Exhale: and find my power.

DAY 9

Listen

A shoot shall come out from the stump of Jesse,
    and a branch shall grow out of his roots.
The spirit of the LORD shall rest on him,
    the spirit of wisdom and understanding,
    the spirit of counsel and might,
    the spirit of knowledge and the fear of the LORD.
        —Isaiah 11:1-2

And again Isaiah says,

"The root of Jesse shall come,
    the one who rises to rule the gentiles;
in him the gentiles shall hope."

May the God of hope fill you with all joy and peace in believing,
so that you may abound in hope by the power of the Holy Spirit.
        —Romans 15:12-13

i am free to look back.

As we see repeated in the Isaiah and Romans passages, the imagery of trees is important to the biblical Advent narrative. The story of Jesus is one that tells of legacy and generations—just like the tree. One tree holds the memory of seasonal flourishing and barrenness while also knowing the growth and tragedies of its environment.

The tree metaphor invites us to imagine the relationship between a deep root and an extended branch. Like generations, trees help us see interconnectedness. We know enough about trees to connect the branch still receiving its nutrients from a root deep in the soil. In this stretch of a tree are hundreds of years of growth and the regular passage of water and hormones.

"The stump of Jesse," or "the root of Jesse," draws us into the importance of generational stories. Imagining Jesse as "root" or "stump" points our minds and spirits toward the deep and historical coming that is held in the emerging of Jesus. Jesse is the father of King David, from whom we get the genealogical lineage of Jesus, and many generations are held in this reference that connects Jesse and Jesus. The invitation of the root of Jesse invites us to go back to where our stories with others first connected. In this image, Advent is drawing us into the connections we have with ancestors and descendants—including rich memories and unknown or fractured relationships.

In our knowing or unknowing, "the Spirit shall rest upon him" reminds us that the interconnectedness of generations is one of the ways we find God. The prophet Isaiah points to the wisdom, understanding, counsel, might, knowledge, and fear that flow from the root to the branch that will grow upward. What has been carried by other leaders is anticipated in Jesus. Many centuries later, Paul ends his letter to the Romans by referring again to this sacred lineage and connecting it to our future hope.

Together in these passages, we hold the story of Jesse's roots, Jesus' power, and hope that will continue to grow in us. One of the reminders of this season is that in birth, we are reminded of where we come from and where our hopes lie. Roots ground us to the connections we have, usually in ways we cannot see. More visibly, stumps are the reminders of places where trees once were, even when growth ends.

The holidays often mean we spend a lot of time gathering with people in configurations of work, social, and family relationships. Some of the stresses of the holidays are because we give our attention to the shallow aspects of our lives and relationships. We focus on where we've been shopping and drama between other people. We can be gracious with ourselves when this happens. *If this is what you need to do to survive, do it!*

Looking back invites us to the source and future of our hope. As you gather with people, what are the values and experiences that bring you together? What is your shared root? How does it connect to what you hope for now?

Breath prayer

Inhale: From my roots,

Exhale: I have hope.

DAY 10

Listen

But do not ignore this one fact, beloved, that with the Lord one day is like a thousand years, and a thousand years are like one day. The Lord is not slow about his promise, as some think of slowness, but is patient with you, not wanting any to perish but all to come to repentance. But the day of the Lord will come like a thief, and then the heavens will pass away with a loud noise, and the elements will be destroyed with fire, and the earth and everything that is done on it will be disclosed. . . .

But, in accordance with his promise, we wait for new heavens and a new earth, where righteousness is at home.

Therefore, beloved, while you are waiting for these things, strive to be found by him at peace, without spot or blemish, and regard the patience of our Lord as salvation.

−2 Peter 3:8-10, 13-15

a prayer desiring to move differently

This passage gives us new ways to think about time and pace. "One day with the Lord is like a thousand years" and "the Lord is not slow but is patient" draw us into a rhythm of God that moves with loving intention. It is contrasted with imagery of God coming as a thief, with a forceful tone of intention referencing fire and noise.

The invitation to us is to "strive to be found by him at peace." The words *strive* and *peace* seem to parallel the different intentions of the previous verses. Striving includes strain and vigor, whereas peace welcomes calmness and alignment. Like other contrasts we are holding in Advent, we can come to ideas and definitions anew. To strive toward peace means exerting ourselves toward a more relational place with God.

Advent gives us permission to move toward God differently, seeking and striving for God in ways that enhance peace. Choose one of the following invitations to attempt a new practice that might reveal God differently for you. Most striving includes a bit of discomfort—reaching for something just out of our regular patterns. Allow your invitation to be a bit uncomfortable.

In your mind and your spirit:

- Make a list of three recent experiences of joy or pleasure. Close your eyes and bring the setting to mind again. Notice what was holy or sacred in each experience.
- Speak aloud as many names of family members as you can recall, living and deceased. End with gratitude for their lives and wisdom.
- When was the last time you heard a meaningful truth? (The kind that make you go *humph* at the end!) Offer a prayer for the person who offered it, the context, and the courage of those now holding it.
- List a series of truths about your family or community (whether positive truths or simply what is). Reread the list, including the word *and* between each statement.

In your body and your spirit:

- Find private space and set an alarm for five minutes. Give yourself permission to relax until you hear the alarm.
- Use your hands to massage your shoulders, hips, and knees. In each of these places, imagine how that body part aids your daily movement, and offer gratitude.

✦ Go outside or look through a window and concentrate on the direction of the wind. If needed, change your direction or gaze to move with it. Let the soles of your feet rest directly on the ground. Ideally, outside in the grass or in the space where you find yourself. Consider what it means to be grounded.

DAY 11

Listen

See, I am sending my messenger to prepare the way before me, and the LORD whom you seek will suddenly come to his temple. The messenger of the covenant in whom you delight—indeed, he is coming, says the LORD of hosts. But who can endure the day of his coming, and who can stand when he appears?

–Malachi 3:1-2

i am free to question.

I highlight this passage to point more largely to the prophet Malachi. We rarely hear or focus on this book, but it serves a very important role in the Advent journey. Malachi, speaking at the very conclusion of the Old Testament, is known as a messenger prophet. There is an intensity and a directness to Malachi, as he seeks to hold the people of Israel accountable to the coming of God. As shown in our passage, the book is a series of prophetic statements paired with questions—a rare combination. Here we see this declaration of the coming of a messenger and this direct question to the listener asking who will stand to endure this coming. This scripture asks, "Are you really ready?"

The entirety of this short book continues in pairs of directives and questions. The questions are bold, requiring the reader to reflect on our individual and collective faithfulness to God and the ways we lean into self-awareness. A few of the questions return prompts of responsibility back to God.

Linger on a few of the questions from the book of Malachi:

> How have we despised your name? (1:6)
> How have we wearied you? (2:17)
> Where is the God of justice? (2:17)
> How have we robbed you? (3:8)
> And how have we spoken against you? (3:13)

In the fifty-five verses that compose this book, there are a total of twenty-two questions similar in style. If held prayerfully, the questions of Malachi can bring us into confessional and lamenting spaces with God. They draw us into accountability, wrestling with our met and unmet needs in our relationship with God. Questions are the foundation of building and sustaining meaningful relationships between people and communities.

Questions serve to gather new information, to clarify existing information, to confirm shared intention, or to inquire about someone else's experience. Curiosity, creativity, and critical thinking all connect to our willingness to question, but I don't think we ask enough questions in our lives. I think this is on purpose.

I think not asking questions reflects our assumed knowledge—we don't ask more questions because we believe we already know the answers. Or we don't ask more questions because we want to be perceived as having more knowledge than we carry. There is arrogance in our certainty. And it often distances us from the possibility of enriched relationships, generative critique, and the process of collaborative idea-making.

In my experiences of spiritual direction, I have witnessed the power of questions to create new learning and growth in a person's spirituality. Our relationships with God include experiences of presence and absence, feeling the spectrum of joy and anger. Most of my sessions include the questions "How are you and God?" and "Have you noticed God recently?," allowing our questions to move past the assumptions of a perfect faith to expressions of an honest relationship. The vulnerability and trust to hold what emerges in questions is sacred. As Malachi models, our willingness to let questions be containers for truth makes our engagement prophetic.

Breath prayer

Inhale: I can hold questions

Exhale: and be faithful.

Listen

Six days before the Passover Jesus came to Bethany, the home of
Lazarus, whom he had raised from the dead. There they gave a dinner for him. Martha served, and Lazarus was one of those reclining
with him. Mary took a pound of costly perfume made of pure nard,
anointed Jesus's feet, and wiped them with her hair. The house was
filled with the fragrance of the perfume. But Judas Iscariot, one of
his disciples (the one who was about to betray him), said, "Why was
this perfume not sold for three hundred denarii and the money given
to the poor?" (He said this not because he cared about the poor but
because he was a thief; he kept the common purse and used to steal
what was put into it.) Jesus said, "Leave her alone. She bought it so
that she might keep it for the day of my burial. You always have the
poor with you, but you do not always have me."

–John 12:1-8

SERMONETTE

Oil and Grace, Tools for Our Faith

Take a minute and dig into the beauty of this passage. Imagine this scene and
walk into Mary and Martha's house with me:

Visualize the warm and inviting images of this banquet in Bethany. The
long wooden table is filled with bread and olives, pitchers with wine and
water. Men are parked along the table benches, and women are circling with
more overflowing plates and cups for communal enjoyment. Surely there are

children peeking in the corner of the doorways and whispering about what they see and hear.

Hear the laughter and chatter as Lazarus and other friends gather to honor Jesus. People are still amazed at the raising of Lazarus and are surely inviting Jesus to tell yet another story or parable. Listen to the sound of celebration in life and the faithfulness that the miracle welcomed.

Take a whiff of the room. You can smell the dusty air and the aroma of fresh bread. In the air is still the stench of Lazarus—his body that was just dead and was prepared with the ointments for burial. The odor of death is met with this strong, exotic, and floral scent of perfume that floods the room.

Mary is not given a voice here, but imagine what words she may be speaking. What does she say while brushing her hair across Christ's feet or in response to Judas's critique? Back in the kitchen, Martha's words are also lost to us. What does she feel and think as the drama unfolds? Is she angry that once again Mary has drawn attention to herself? Are her hopes for this meal disrupted?

Feel the weight of the tension in the air. Faithfulness and greed. Rowdiness and voicelessness. The joy and abundance held with the pending plot to kill Jesus. The simultaneous smells of life and death. This narrative looks backward and forward at the same time.

Where do you feel yourself identifying? In the joy, in the tension, in the silence, in the blessing? As you open your eyes, the reality is clear that life with Jesus, then and now, is complex and draws all parts of us in.

Of all the profound imagery of this passage, I am most struck by its smells. You can likely recall an experience of smell that floods the mind with arresting memories of a person, place, or event. Olfaction, emotion, and memory share closely networked real estate in the brain's limbic system. Our sense of smell relates closely to how we experience life and how we process significant memories. I have had foul odors from an unseen dumpster literally stop me in my tracks because they conjure sights and sounds I experienced as a teenager on a life-changing visit to a Honduran slum. Similarly, someone wearing the fragrance that my grandmother wore can bring immediate joy to my spirit.

Wine, death, perfume, hot sun, greed, bread. It seems like the smells fully capture the complexity of this experience. What is it about smell? Those that please and those that repulse? Those that delight and those that distance? Those that anticipate and those that repel?

In the previous chapter of John's gospel, Jesus arrived at the tomb where Lazarus was buried. It's important to remember that he was fully dead and buried, with all the spices and oils and cloths used to wrap his corpse. By the time Jesus got there, Lazarus had been in the tomb for four days. It's likely that even several days later at this dinner, he still stunk. Even stronger in the air, though, may have been the odor of death reclining upon Jesus. Jesus quickly begins to plan his own burial, and his words reflect the dark, tragic mood and air that surround him.

Then . . . as smells do . . . a new smell enters and begins to mingle with the first. This costly, satisfying aroma of perfume begins to weave itself into the ordinary, gritty death funk that was lingering. Against everything that is right, Mary empties the vase of oil on the feet of Jesus. She should have been ashamed of her actions.

To think she was like the disciples in authority and could anoint Jesus! She should have felt ashamed. To expend such an extravagant oil without thought of the poor! She should have been ashamed of this waste. To counter-culturally expose her hair! She should have been ashamed of her body. Mary's actions are astounding, embarrassing, intimate, uncomfortable . . . shameful.

But Jesus says, "Leave her alone." Affirming her faithfulness and inviting her humble blessing. Is Jesus' response what grace smells like?

Mary is shameless as she steps far outside of what is expected of her, teetering on the edge of scandal. Mary shows her love for Christ in a bold and confident display of affection, pouring out her heart as she mourns what Jesus will soon endure. Mary has heard Jesus' teachings and his warnings about the path he must travel. She weeps at the sacrifice of almighty God for her own self. As she lovingly prepares Jesus for death, she grieves openly and shares in his suffering.

Judas, experiencing something very different, is resentful. Our scripture explains Judas's life as one of betrayal of trust and hoarding of treasure. Instead of following the example that Christ sets, Judas resists generosity. Why was this perfume not sold for three hundred denarii and the money given to the poor? John makes it clear that Judas's question of Mary is not inspired by concern for the poor. Judas is uncomfortable with Mary's display of devotion. Where Mary gives, Judas hoards. Where Mary sacrifices financially, Judas seeks self-benefit. *And yet what Judas critiques as waste is the greatest gift that Mary can give.* Not expensive perfume or money but the offering of her very life, stripped of all masks, given in service to Christ.

Are they graceful or shameful? Are we? Who gets to decide? It's all uncomfortable and perfectly complicated. Shame creeps in just like this. Shame is deep and messy, no perfect black-and-white answers—all hues of grey to muddle through. If we began to name and uproot some of our own shame, it would sound just like the complexity of this dinner scene. We walk around with shame—about our habits, our limitations, our bodies, our past. It lingers like funk in the air. Then we get whiffs of fragrant grace—warm community that greets us each Sunday, Jesus asserting "Leave her alone" when people question our deepest sacrifice, the father who welcomes and loves both of his sons.

Trying to find Jesus in the middle of our shame feels just like these competing smells. See, smells don't replace each other—they contrast one another. The smell of that perfume was not to counteract death, erase death's smell, or try to overpower its stench. It was intended as a scent to smell at the same time you smell the scent of death. This is the uncomfortable and complicated beauty of how we become released from shame. The contrast in these smells expands the truth about our everyday life.

It is while we smell our mistakes that we can also smell grace. There is no middle ground, no "safe" offering. It is while we push through the darkness that we can choose to trust God fully. It is while we sit with our pain that we access our power. As much as we want Mary's perfume to wash away the funk, death and life exist together. One does not exist without the other. This is the beauty of our story as Christians, and this is our hope.

IT IS THE NIGHT

Dwelling in the truth

The second line of "O Holy Night" offers the central and obvious truth of this Christmas song. "It is the night of our dear Savior's birth" names realities of the event and its location rather matter-of-factly. The truth of the night and birth also invite our own awareness of this experience. For some, it becomes visceral that we are in a dark transition. For others, birth holds the vulnerability of life. There is capacity for anticipation, joy, worry, fear—when we let ourselves confront it.

Most simply, this season of Advent asks us to slow down and be attentive to what is most true in our spirits and in those we share communities with. Only from this place of dwelling do we know what we need in the coming of God so that we can be attuned to it as it appears. "It is the night" nudges us to an honesty with where we are, dwelling in what is true—whatever that may be. How do we dwell in what is true? How do we also stay present to what is coming?

a prayer for calling it what it is

The italic text is from author and poet Pádraig Ó Tuama in his book In the Shelter *and highlights the theme of welcoming that which we may fear. The words in between are prayerful.*

Much of our desire to not-name a place is because we fear that in naming it we are giving it power, and by giving it power we are saying we may not escape. It's a valid fear.

God of power, we know that we wander through life ascribing meaning and power to things from our humanity. Some of the powers we have enabled are bigger than us and our fears. It's scary, and we know its okay to be scared. Call us by our name. And remind us that you have already named all that is divine.

There are some suburbs of hell that we wish we'd never visited, and we neither want to give nor remember a name. And so, through energy, prayer, determination, or other hopes, we refuse to give a name to the place we resent.

God who remembers, parts of our memories and our truths are difficult to enter. Places in our mind are charged, and others are completely numb. We need to know that when we find ourselves in the frightening or infuriating parts of ourselves, we can also still find you.

To name something can be to call it into being, and we do not wish to call certain things into any kind of being. Hello to this awful truth: it is here anyway.[7]

God who is also here, I simply want to be more honest—with myself and with you. Help me learn a rhythm this season that invites my truth. Give me peace for all that I encounter. Guide me toward the places I can name and still hold my peace. Restore to me the power I have conceded to my fears.

DAY 14

Listen

Then Jerusalem and all Judea and all the region around the Jordan were going out to him, and they were baptized by him in the River Jordan, confessing their sins. . . .

[John said,] "I baptize you with water for repentance, but the one who is coming after me is more powerful than I, and I am not worthy to carry his sandals. He will baptize you with the Holy Spirit and fire."

—Matthew 3:5-6, 11

in the waters, i am free.

For a season of my life, I lived in a small waterside village in the Dominican Republic. This was more than fifteen years ago, but I can still sit still enough to hear the harmony of the waves. The warm waters of that land introduced me to a God I hadn't known before, alongside a new culture and language.

Throughout biblical narratives, water is a symbol of God's presence and power across time and place. Some of my favorite words are from Rachel Held Evans in *Searching for Sunday* as she describes the waters through creation, where God first hovered over the dark waters, blessing them. Through the Nile waters that carried Moses, the tears of Jesus, and the instruction to go out and baptize the whole world—every drop is holy.

The Matthew 3 scripture continues the sermon of John the Baptist, preparing the people of Israel for a powerful coming of Christ. As a leader, John is a bridge between generations. His message is one of meaningful preparation and intentional transition, ways we also understand Advent. He ends his words with the ritual of baptism, a practice we continue to connect with the bringing in of new life with Christ. While these themes align, baptism and the use of holy water is not a symbol we regularly connect with the Advent or Christmas season.

With its use in John's declaration, I hear baptism with a new meaning. He gives voice to baptism as a transitional space. John's hope is that the waters of baptism will facilitate our passage from one way of being to another. And the actual waters are an in-between with importance and opportunity, like Advent itself.

Just as we want to fly through Advent to Christmas, so we want to fly through baptism. We move through the ritual for the celebration of emerging, missing our presence *in* the water as a location unto itself.

Our bodies know the meaning of presence in water better than our minds do. Before birth, babies linger in amniotic fluid that the body of the birthing person produces. The fluid creates a shield of impact to protect from injury and helps to maintain body temperature through different seasons, growing with the belly and the baby to account for size. Amniotic fluid begins as 98 percent water and functions as a catalyst for growth of lungs and digestion as babies breathe and swallow it. Our lives begin knowing water as a liminal space. A dwelling place for transition, the waters of pregnancy are a location of exponential growth and being.

Is Advent a liminal body of water, inviting us to be held in this dark and holy place? Womb-like, can Advent be a time and space where we let ourselves transition to new ways of being? Will we let this season be a season, without seeking to jump quickly out of these waters?

Breath prayer

Inhale: **Hold me in the waters,**

Exhale: **and fill me with your Spirit.**

DAY 15

Listen

Be patient, therefore, brothers and sisters, until the coming of the Lord. The farmer waits for the precious crop from the earth, being patient with it until it receives the early and the late rains. You also must be patient. Strengthen your hearts, for the coming of the Lord is near.

–James 5:7-8

i am free to be still.

Be patient. Wait. Expect. Anticipate. Advent requires these responses of us as we continue to wait for Christmas. These responses require work. Being patient requires us to manage the natural anxieties of our bodies. Waiting means delaying desires and needs for what still waits ahead of us. The concepts of expecting and anticipating expect us to move counterculturally against high-speed realities. The work of waiting during the season of Advent is not easy. It is not simple or natural.

In today's passage, James draws us to patience with the image of a farmer waiting on a crop, dependent only on the rain. This farmer has likely tilled and seeded, watered, and weeded. They are simply waiting for the crop to sprout. And no meaningful actions can be taken to quicken the sprout—this is waiting.

I am personally quite impatient. My internal motivation is mostly in overdrive. And as an older millennial, technology has led me to believe that waiting is inefficient. Sometimes I have to manufacture ways to distract myself by creating new short-term hopes that precede the thing I am actually waiting for. When I am lacking creativity during a writing project, I create a task of formatting my documents for when the words come. (And then I likely adjust the formatting again.) If I'm honest, I create more doing than is congruent with a sense of waiting.

Reading this passage from James allows me to receive the invitation to wait in a more healthy way. We often believe that for something to turn out good, we need to work more or work faster. Here, there is no more work for the farmer to do. There is only the waiting—for the rain and the sprouting. The farmer has taken all the appropriate steps that could lead to a sprouting crop—what remains now is the work of the soil and the rain.

More tangibly, we plant seeds like advocacy and activism so that crops of peace instead of war or joy instead of grief may grow. The urgency of needs, the limits of resources, the hopes we long for challenge how we differentiate work, impatience, and stillness. Yes, there is work, and sometimes there is urgent work. When do we let stillness help us see the work happening in the soil?

If the farmer embraces stillness, they can more easily witness the work of the soil, the rain, and the crop. We, too, can be still in our waiting.

Breath prayer

Inhale and *exhale* with each phrase:

Be still and know that I am God.

Be still and know that I am.

Be still and know that I.

Be still and know that.

Be still and know.

Be still and.

Be still.

Be.

DAY 16

Listen

Be patient, therefore, brothers and sisters, until the coming of the Lord. The farmer waits for the precious crop from the earth, being patient with it until it receives the early and the late rains. You also must be patient. Strengthen your hearts, for the coming of the Lord is near.

–James 5:7-8

a prayer to celebrate the goodness i cannot see

Unheard prayers for your health and strength.
The hope of your grandparents.
Affirmations of your work in meetings you don't attend.

The consistency of sunrises.
A God who listens.
Safety while you slept last night.

Loving children who apologize and help your child back up in the middle of recess.
Farmers who carefully tend the vegetables that come your way.
Nurses who put a rush on tests for faster results.

Friends who trust your mistakes without response.
The sacrifice of your parents.
Imagination. Vulnerability. Silence.

That inner voice that reminds you that you are powerful.
The air of peace that lets grief settle in.
Forgiveness that reshapes your love for yourself and others.

Faith.
Hope.
Love.

God of the darkness and the unknown, you give us so many gifts to embrace what is not seen. You affirm divine presence beyond our vision and knowing. Help us look and listen into the unknown, trusting that good gifts will be revealed. Relieve our anxieties in our scurried searching, and restore a patient hope. As we wait like the farmer anticipating the precious crops in the earth, remind us that seeds break open, rains will come, and sprouts will emerge. Amen.

DAY 17

Listen

Happy are those whose help is the God of Jacob,
    whose hope is in the LORD their God,
who made heaven and earth,
    the sea, and all that is in them;
who keeps faith forever;
    who executes justice for the oppressed;
    who gives food to the hungry.
        —Psalm 146:5-7

i am free in complicated feelings.

This chapter of Psalms is one of the last. And like the ends of all other great pieces of writing or music, it ends in fullness. Beginning and ending with hallelujah, it closes with grand declarations of the goodness of God in a spirit of joy or happiness.

I'll be honest and admit that high joy is not my thing. I don't dislike it or avoid it, but my own temperament holds tension more easily than full joy. So in the beginning of the passage, the word *happy* doesn't resonate with me. Then, when I reread this passage, I see it as a complicated form of happy.

Our social concept of happiness often requires our ability to point to something tangible that is delightful, positive, or optimistic. For example, we are given permission to celebrate and be happy when we buy our first house. A standard of happy is set by this act, and other realities do not equate to happiness. Psalm 146 complicates that expectation.

The psalmist connects this *happy* with those whose help or hope is in God, not simply the tangible forms of happy we can point to right now. Verse 5 names "happy are those whose help is the God of Jacob, whose hope is in the Lord their God." The scope of God is defined by the realm of things within heaven and earth, the sea and forever. Happy, from the psalmist's perspective, is expansive and distant, in places beyond our reach. This closing psalm expands the definition of happy that we approach it with. Happy here is not quite present or proximate—it is held in the not yet. This is a long-term happy, dependent on the vast help and hope within God's realm.

The Hebrew translation of the word *happy*, *ash'rei*, is often translated into the English word *blessed*. It is used throughout Psalms, Proverbs, and Job to describe a type of relationship with God where we live into blessings as we persist with God.

- Ash'rei are those who take refuge in God (Psalms 2:12; 34:8)
- Ash'rei is the nation whose God is Yhwh (Psalms 33:12; 144:15)
- Ash'rei are those who put their trust in Yhwh (Psalms 40:4; 84:12)
- Ash'rei are those whom God chooses to draw near (Psalm 65:4)
- Ash'rei are those who know the joyful sound (Psalm 89:15)
- Ash'rei are those whose strength is in Yhwh (Psalm 84:5)
- Ash'rei are those who find wisdom and understanding (Proverbs 3:13)
- Ash'rei are those who keep God's ways (Proverbs 8:32)
- Ash'rei are those who listen, watch, and wait for Yhwh (Proverbs 8:34)
- Ash'rei is one who is corrected by God (Job 5:17)

Blessedness reframes happiness, and *ash'rei* invites us into a happiness of God. Ash'rei is about relationship—being attentive and trusting, sharing truth and wisdom. This relationship of blessing develops over time with care and commitment. Moving beyond our common notion of happiness to be physically and emotionally accessible, we hear the invitation of blessedness to sustained and involved relationship. This is the invitation of Advent.

To be blessed, we are called to understand something different about who we are. It is a different sense of time than a moment or a season; blessedness is about what will be true in and through our lives as we walk with God.

Perhaps happiness or blessing is our ability to point to an enduring relationship with God where we expect something we can't yet see. And we celebrate the ways we know ourselves because of it.

Breath prayer

Inhale: I am blessed.

Exhale: As I am.

DAY 18

Listen

We declare to you what was from the beginning, what we have heard, what we have seen with our eyes, what we have looked at and touched with our hands, concerning the word of life—this life was revealed, and we have seen it and testify to it and declare to you the eternal life that was with the Father and was revealed to us—what we have seen and heard we also declare to you so that you also may have fellowship with us, and truly our fellowship is with the Father and with his Son Jesus Christ. . . .

If we say that we have no sin, we deceive ourselves, and the truth is not in us. If we confess our sins, he who is faithful and just will forgive us our sins and cleanse us from all unrighteousness.

–1 John 1:1-3, 8-9

SERMONETTE

Confession as a Dwelling Practice

From kindergarten to eighth grade, I attended a Catholic school in the Hyde Park area of Chicago. It was a small school and required that students and their families participate in the life of the parish. In addition to education, St. Thomas taught me elements of community and mission. I attended mass every week (I can still completely recite the liturgy of the eucharist) and helped stock the food pantry.

The building was old, and like most Catholic churches included all the beautiful elements of ritual: rickety kneeling benches, several fonts holding holy water, captivating stained glass windows, and a sacred altar area that had more detail than I was ever able to take in. In the back of the sanctuary, a large, seemingly person-sized box protruded from the wall. The confessional had two doors—one where ordinary people went in, and the other where the priest entered. Because I was not Catholic, I was never allowed to participate in the act of confession, and the confessional was a very protected space that we were not allowed to joke about or play around. That didn't matter. I snuck in a few times— because it was spooky, and somebody had told me not to. Sneaking in, I realized that this was a space for conversation, but before that realization I'd thought of it as a place where people went if they killed someone or committed robbery.

When we hear the word *confession*, I think that many of our minds go to places similar to the confessional in my old school. It's mysterious, protected, emerges out of nowhere, and is not well understood. Formally, confession is the spiritual practice that allows us to enter into the grace and mercy of God in such a way that we experience forgiveness and healing for the sins and sorrows of the past. More simply, confession is what sits with us in the stillness of any silence. It is the space where truth is naked and free.

Coming to the practice of confession as non-Catholics is difficult. For many of us, our theology doesn't invite us to have this conversation with a priest, but our practices don't help us sit in that stillness either. Inherent in confession is the reality that we make mistakes—that we hurt others, creation, and even ourselves. In that mistake-making, injury occurs. Life is destroyed, feelings are damaged, people are left unseen. Many of us do not live with this reality well, and to be honest, most of our institutions completely ignore it. Our relationship with mistake-making is underdeveloped. .

Those who lived in the biblical context did not have this problem. The awareness and navigation of sin was ongoing. In the book of 1 John, the writer helps us navigate our relationship with sin: If we say we are without it, we are lying. If we admit our sins, God will forgive and cleanse.

John is writing this, bearing witness to the first century of Christianity as a time of strife and the splitting of some Christian communities over differences. First John is written to dissenters desiring to split off because of disagreements especially about the person of Jesus and the nature of the Christian life. These dissenters denied that Jesus was really human and believed that they followed the model of a spiritual Christ. As Christ is "heavenly," sinless, and wise—they believed the same of themselves. What we have in 1 John, though, is not an attack against these questioners, but a positive appeal to readers to embrace the incarnate Christ and enter into fellowship with Father and Son.

If there were an equation here, it would read confession equals forgiveness plus healing. The spiritual practice we are being invited into includes these two major elements. Forgiveness is our admission of wrongdoing, and healing is our letting go of being wronged. Confession relies on both of these processes.

Forgiveness is at the heart of the Christian faith. "Father, forgive them," Jesus prayed from the cross. "I believe in the forgiveness of sins," affirms the ancient baptismal creed. And as the writer of Ephesians urges us, "Forgive one another as God in Christ has forgiven you" (Ephesians 4:32).

If we are honest, we have to admit that we do not see much forgiveness, not real forgiveness. Forgiveness in the New Testament sense is not a superficial event. It is not merely a willingness to "let bygones be bygones" or to throw up one's hands with an "Ah, forget it, life must go on" attitude. In the New Testament, forgiveness is about making what is tragically broken right again. The Hebrew and Greek words translated in our Scriptures mean atone, let go, lift up, or be gracious. Forgiveness is about a deep healing, a thorough repair of broken relationships, a removal of the poison that destroys love and harmony, a restoration of wholeness and open trust.

Throughout the world, the month of June is set aside to celebrate and honor the value of LGBTQ persons in our cities and communities. Many of our communities host parades and events for those who identify as LGBTQ and their allies who love and support them. I read an article of a church in the Philippines who chose to respond to the relationship between the church and this marginalized community with forgiveness. They stood at the entrance of the event with signs of apology. Not with a trivial awareness of how the church has inflicted pain, but with acknowledgment of deep wrongs for the sake of restoration, offering the words "We are here to apologize for the ways we as Christians have harmed the LGBTQ community."

I'm sorry for not listening.

I'm sorry I have looked down on you instead of honoring your humanity.

I'm sorry for hiding behind religion when I was really scared.

As any good therapist will tell you, you cannot heal what you do not acknowledge. What you do not consciously acknowledge will remain in control from within, festering and destroying you and those around you. In the Gospel of Thomas, Jesus teaches, "If you bring forth that which is within you, it will save you. If you do not bring it forth, it will destroy you" (saying 70).[8]

Confession begins with sitting in truth and naming our own wrongdoings. Healing forgiveness happens as we accept the apologies of ourselves and one another. The words "I forgive you" are healing words. In between, there is sometimes a need for justice, and that's a whole other sermon.

In *Celebration of Disciplines*, theologian Richard Foster talks about the practice of confession, suggesting we treat it not as an event but as a deliberate framing of our life in an honest and open manner—accepting truth and not trying to cover things up. A life that integrated confession would live authentically into both "I'm sorrys" and "I forgive yous." This takes work—late night talks with your loved ones, extra conversation spaces outside of worship and Sunday school, giving yourself grace as God would.

Once a year, on a Wednesday, we mix ashes with oil. We light candles and confess to one another and to God that we have sinned by what we have done and what we have left undone. We tell the truth. Then we smear ashes on our foreheads, collectively acknowledging that "we are dust and to dust we will return." Our default is to relegate the practice of confession to this one event as we enter Lent, treating it just like that same strange box that protruded from the back of St. Thomas. Yet we are always dust, working our way into more honest relationship and finding the courage to dwell there.

IN SIN AND ERROR PINING

Longing for a Savior

There are traditional weekly themes of Advent: hope, peace, joy, love. If you are following them in other places, you will notice that love is typically the theme at this time in the season. These themes seek to highlight gifts that come with the arrival of Jesus. Yet inherent in the coming of these gifts is the reality that they are not fully present with us.

Despair, war, oppression, sadness, fear, grief are the themes we don't name explicitly that still join us in this season. "Long lay the world in sin and error pining" describes a world that still longs for a Savior and the fullness of God's love. As we move into the fourth week of Advent, we continue with scriptures that remind us of a coming God, without yet approaching the passages of the Christmas narrative. In touch with our deepest needs, there is longing in our hearts, our communities, and our world.

Listen

The materialism in this book lives in the flesh of these women's lives: the exhaustion we feel in our bones at the end of the day, the fire we feel in our hearts when we are insulted, the knife we feel in our backs when we are betrayed, the nausea we feel in our bones when we are afraid, even the hunger we feel between our hips when we long to be touched.

I am not talking here about some lazy faith, where we resign ourselves to the tragic splittings in our lives with an upward turn of the hands or a vicious beating of our breasts. I am talking about believing that we have the power to actually transform our experience, change our lives, save our lives. Otherwise, why this book? It is the faith of activists I am talking about.[9]

—Cherríe Moraga, preface to *This Bridge Called My Back*

in the dark, they are free.

This Bridge Called My Back is an anthology of writing from "radical women of color" first published in 1981 as they sought to complicate the narrative of feminism in the United States. They bring experiences that reflect their lives as women, women of color, mothers, refugees and immigrants, lesbians, and working women. They talk of straddling worlds, translating cultures, and bridging gaps of understanding, even when they are the most marginalized person in a given context. Everything about the concept of this book expresses darkness, from identities to social locations, and it is a celebration of power.

From voices that extend around the globe, these writers regain ownership of experiences that were merely talked about before. *This Bridge Called My Back* is a convergence of collective power, one that for more than forty years has been a resource from women who are finding their way through the dark in solidarity. The anthology holds together examples of the lived experiences of authentic and powerful Brown and Black women in longing and suffering. In her preface, Cherríe Moraga uses the felt realities known through exhaustion, fire, knifing, nausea, and hunger to remind us of the humanity and courage in these narratives.

Moraga's second paragraph in today's text explores the impact of making space for the women's textured voices and truth telling. This text becomes an act of faith, weaving together their idea of faith as active and powerful and the ways it becomes manifest in the text.

Our theological and social concepts of the dark overlay our perceptions. Sometimes we look into the dark with assumptions that everything within it is void—powerless and voiceless. People and situations that own or celebrate darkness are lumped into this mis-categorization. People in dark places can be powerful; they can articulate bold faith, and they can act in creative and sacred ways.

I honor the women of color who stand in some of the darkest nights of our realities—grateful for their flesh and their faith. I believe God blesses their darkness. I believe God rushes to the location of darkness to sustain the sacred in it. I believe God's promises begin in the darkest places.

Breath prayer

Inhale: Darkness and power breathe together.

Exhale: This breath starts in God.

Listen

As it is written in the prophet Isaiah,

"See, I am sending my messenger ahead of you,
who will prepare your way,
the voice of one crying out in the wilderness:
'Prepare the way of the Lord;
make his paths straight.'"
—Mark 1:2-3

with fragmented hopes, i am free.

Whenever I hear the phrase "Prepare the way of the Lord," I am captured by an overwhelming visual. I see masses of people, not crowded but linear and curving, as far as my eyes can detect. They are present and focused in one direction, their energies all flowing toward a shared center. This image gives me comfort; it feels supportive. These folks feel like my ancestors. This is the image I hold for preparation.

Preparation sometimes looks like full-on event planning where we can perfectly manipulate logistics, timing, and experience. Many beautiful days and weekends are planned this way. But the preparation in this season of Advent is deeper and richer. It's the kind of preparation that began generations ago, with foresight for how things could be. This preparation is aspirational and imaginative and seeks the best for people and creation.

I never met my maternal grandmother, Margarette. She died when my mother was still young, so what I know of her comes from stories. I've sought opportunities to listen to those who hold them, and they talk about her passion for ministry and education, focused on children and their formation. She was a beautiful Black woman in her prime during the 1940s. At a time of limited access to higher and graduate education, Grandma Margarette started a seminary education in what I believe was a response to a call from God. I see much of my own vocation in her and resonate with whatever God was doing in her heart. And I often wonder how her desire and efforts prepared the way for me.

Like our connections to our ancestors, this preparation is not complete. It comes to us in fragments—stories, scents, memories, and evenings of tears. It is prompted by a word or song, a photo, or the new facial expression of a child.

Neither is this preparation prescribed; we do not know how it will unfold. Yet it is intentional. The prophecy of Isaiah tells of the how, not the what. Further along, John the Baptist says in verses 7 and 8, "The one who is more powerful than I is coming after me; I am not worthy to stoop down and untie the strap of his sandals. I have baptized you with water, but he will baptize you with the Holy Spirit." Power and Spirit define the hope and anticipation without details of how that will be made known.

I cling to the wisdom of Rosemarie Freeney Harding and her daughter Rachel Harding in their book *Remnants: A Memoir of Spirit, Activism, and Mothering* as they piece together personal and collective memories of love and grief, spirituality and racial trauma, ritual, and wisdom. I was introduced to Rosemarie and her husband Vincent Harding as I learned of their involvement in the Mennonite church and the civil rights movement during the 1960s. Like the remnants of fabric that compose beautiful quilts, these pieces shaped Rosemarie's powerful life of loving her children, fighting for civil rights, and nurturing families toward well-being.

This season of Advent is preparation—ancient and deep, fragmented and organic, with unfulfilled hopes that our grandmothers and other ancestors held. Advent prepares us for a relationship with Jesus that also unfolds in fragments. I think preparation is possible and maybe even complete while the process itself is incomplete. While we can't manufacture what this will fully become, we continue to witness and gather remnants that are parts of the whole.

Breath prayer

Inhale: My hope can be in pieces,

Exhale: and my path is still whole.

Listen

Rejoice always, pray without ceasing, give thanks in all circumstances, for this is the will of God in Christ Jesus for you. Do not quench the Spirit. Do not despise prophecies, but test everything; hold fast to what is good; abstain from every form of evil.

May the God of peace himself sanctify you entirely, and may your spirit and soul and body be kept sound and blameless at the coming of our Lord Jesus Christ. The one who calls you is faithful, and he will do this.

—1 Thessalonians 5:16-24

i am free to be authentic.

If you are like me, you just let out a big sigh. This scripture is stressful.

Let's add a little context. This passage comes at the end of 1 Thessalonians as Paul is offering final words to the church. The Thessalonians were an early group of believers in Jesus who gathered not many years after his death and resurrection. They were a community transitioning from belief in many gods, facing persecution from these changed beliefs, and experiencing some anxiety over why Jesus hadn't returned yet.

The Thessalonians ask questions that are likely quite familiar: How do we understand why Jesus hasn't saved us yet? How do we continue to have faith without the presence of God we hoped for? How long will we have to endure this way?

The previous chapters in 1 Thessalonians highlight ways that they might be encouraged, be faithful, and continue together as a body. With a pastoral tone, Paul offers ways they might live faithfully, care for one another, and build community.

In comparison, I find this passage overwhelming and unrealistic. *Rejoice always, pray without ceasing, give thanks in all circumstances, hold fast to what is good; abstain from every form of evil*—I don't find these invitations practical or helpful to the reality of the world as I experience it and my authentic journey with God in it. Rejoicing, prayer, and thanks don't match every facet of my relationship with God. An honest relationship with God is complicated. Or at least, mine is. Which means I give myself permission to feel the anger and disappointment in my delayed expectations.

I want to believe that this passage is an overexaggeration of what Paul actually meant. After all, Paul's admonitions in this passage are the closing remarks to ideas he expanded on previously. These words are being said as a friend exits the door after a long visit together—they're the condensed, pocket-size version of a three-hour conversation. It seems more realistic that these are not literal expectations but pumped-up summaries akin to "You know what to do when it gets hard" and "You can do this!"

The very last sentence is perhaps the actual intent of Paul's blessing to the Thessalonians: *The one who calls you is faithful, and he will do this.* Whew. *The one who calls you is faithful, and he will do this.* The reminder to this faithful community is to trust that their God will also be faithful. In this Advent season and our own recognition of the deep needs for God in the world, these words feel like hope.

Instead of the heavy lift of this passage, I wonder if we can hold this invitation: *Do what you can to stay in conversation with God. Do it as much as you can, with honest intention from your spirit. Know that God will always meet you there.*

Breath prayer

Inhale: I can pause,

Exhale: and offer what I have in this moment.

Listen

The spirit of the Lord GOD is upon me
    because the LORD has anointed me;
he has sent me to bring good news to the oppressed,
    to bind up the brokenhearted,
to proclaim liberty to the captives
    and release to the prisoners,
to proclaim the year of the LORD's favor
    and the day of vengeance of our God,
    to comfort all who mourn,
to provide for those who mourn in Zion—
    to give them a garland instead of ashes,
the oil of gladness instead of mourning,
    the mantle of praise instead of a faint spirit.
They will be called oaks of righteousness,
    the planting of the LORD, to display his glory. . . .

For I, the LORD, love justice,
    I hate robbery and wrongdoing;
I will faithfully give them their recompense,
    and I will make an everlasting covenant with them.
Their descendants shall be known among the nations
    and their offspring among the peoples;
all who see them shall acknowledge
    that they are a people whom the LORD has blessed.
                 —Isaiah 61:1-3, 8-9

a prayer for the Spirit's freedom

Familiar words from the prophet Isaiah and later from Jesus, these words come at a historical moment of important transition for Israel. Isaiah speaks this passage after their exile as they begin to rebuild their land. Within the actions and thinking of rebuilding, God as "the Spirit of the LORD" is a grand declaration of promise, justice, hope, and anticipation. The prophet is nudging the people to remember that God is destined to transform their reality. For us, Advent prepares us for the necessary transformation that is coming in Christ. I offer a litany in the same spirit of the prophet Isaiah's reminder:

The Spirit of the Lord is upon those in unhoused communities.
The Spirit of the Lord is upon our colleague experiencing domestic violence.
The Spirit of the Lord is upon the couple who have chosen to abort
their pregnancy.
The Spirit of the Lord is upon our undocumented neighbor.
The Spirit of the Lord is upon the pastor who has lost their faith.
The Spirit of the Lord is upon our trans uncle.
The Spirit of the Lord is upon the global farmer seeking to protect his land.
The Spirit of the Lord is upon our atheist family member.
The Spirit of the Lord is upon those burdened by shame.
The Spirit of the Lord is upon our sibling who is bipolar.
The Spirit of the Lord is upon parents of children murdered by the police.
The Spirit of the Lord is upon the teenager experimenting with drugs.
The Spirit of the Lord is upon the one who survived.
The Spirit of the Lord is upon the family burdened by trauma.
The Spirit of the Lord is upon the oppressed, the brokenhearted,
and the captive.

Breath prayer

Inhale and exhale with the Spirit.

DAY 23

Listen

Sing aloud, O daughter Zion;
    shout, O Israel!
Rejoice and exult with all your heart,
    O daughter Jerusalem!
The LORD has taken away the judgments against you;
    he has turned away your enemies.
The king of Israel, the LORD, is in your midst;
    you shall fear disaster no more.
On that day it shall be said to Jerusalem:
"Do not fear, O Zion;
    do not let your hands grow weak.
The LORD, your God, is in your midst,
    a warrior who gives victory;
he will rejoice over you with gladness;
    he will renew you in his love;
he will exult over you with loud singing
    as on a day of festival." . . .

At that time I will bring you home,
    at the time when I gather you;
for I will make you renowned and praised
    among all the peoples of the earth,
when I restore your fortunes
    before your eyes, says the LORD.
        –Zephaniah 3:14-18, 20

i am free to worry and hope.

At this point in Advent and Christmas, our lives and our spirits are full, and we may feel weary of the waiting and exhausted by all the flurry of the season. And the mixed messages of these two seasons have reached their maximum point of conflict—do I give in to the despair in my heart, or do I give voice to joy?

How are we supposed to rejoice when our hearts ache? What songs of gladness should we sing when fatigue, anger, or fear darken our lives? Are we supposed to come to God with only parts of ourselves?

Zephaniah doesn't respond to these questions lightly. An Old Testament prophet familiar with corruption and injustice in Judah, he speaks with an awareness of the ways that the oppressed are ashamed and fearful while leaders continue in power hoarding and selfishness. Straight from the passage we hear disaster and victory, shame and renown, gathering and restoring.

This sermon does not come from a prophet who declares an end to all fears and a conclusive rejoicing from the people. Just as our days are not fully light or fully dark, the reality of some hope and some worry is complicated. And while there aren't direct correlations between our world and Zephaniah's, we can relate to the challenging contrasts.

There is both deep compassion around us *and* profound injustice. We see generosity in toy drives and the tragedies of diminishing mental health facilities. Neither is more important or powerful, nor do they cancel each other out. With words repeated in verses 15 and 17, Zephaniah reminds the believer, "The LORD, your God, is in your midst," affirming God's attention to tragedy and restoration. In the strength of a warrior image, the passage ends by speaking God's commitment to restoration to both the broken and the unjust.

While God sees it and is committed to restoration, brokenness and injustice persist.

As I write this, I don't have a clean or easy answer to where an honest Advent finds us. And I don't feel the burden of finding one. I feel aware of a deep longing to give relief to those who are hurting, a belabored hope from heavy hearts, and the lingering of a God who cares. And this feels honest and true. And this is where we meet God—not in singular but layered truths.

I think about other ways we try to make sense of this, ways we experience layered truths. The arts often express the layers in ways our words cannot hold. Sitting at a piano, we can hit two or three random keys—B, G#, and C—and they make a distorted sound similar to when our spirits hold the layers of fatigue, anger, and fear. Painting a canvas, we can overlap the colors red, blue, and yellow and resonate with the nondistinctive brightness and darkness in the same ways that longing, hope, lingering feel in our hearts. The notes and the colors—they fill the air and the canvas, sometimes making something new or revealing the discord of their togetherness.

God and the prophet whom God sends recognize the irregular piano chord and the muddled paint canvases that we carry in our hearts.

"The Lord, your God, is in your midst."

God also agreed to being present, inhabiting the space of our truths.

Breath prayer

Inhale: I was not made to be simple.

Exhale: God, inhabit all of me.

DAY 24

Listen

He has told you, O mortal, what is good;
    and what does the Lord require of you
but to do justice, and to love kindness,
    and to walk humbly with your God?

—Micah 6:8

Blessed are the poor in spirit, for theirs is the kingdom of heaven.
Blessed are those who mourn, for they will be comforted.
Blessed are the meek, for they will inherit the earth.
Blessed are those who hunger and thirst for righteousness, for they
    will be filled.
Blessed are the merciful, for they will receive mercy.
Blessed are the pure in heart, for they will see God.
Blessed are the peacemakers, for they will be called children of God.
Blessed are those who are persecuted for the sake of righteousness,
    for theirs is the kingdom of heaven.
Blessed are you when people revile you and persecute you and utter
    all kinds of evil against you falsely on my account. Rejoice and be
    glad, for your reward is great in heaven, for in the same way they
    persecuted the prophets who were before you.

—Matthew 5:3-12

SERMONETTE

God's Hope for the Future

The setting of Micah 6 is a court case, one where the hills and the mountains have been called to serve as the jury. The suit has been brought forth by God against Israel for breaking their covenant. The accusations include phrases like "images and idols," "pampered children," and "devised wickedness."

On the defendant's side is Israel, complaining that God is responsible for all the current disasters. And with long necks of selfishness and arrogance, the people of Israel peer at their neighboring cities and in the back of their minds say, "Well, their God must be better since they have more bounty and more safety."

And God, as plaintiff, begins opening statements. We don't hear words of anger or a last warning, but a heartfelt plea: "O my people, what have I done to you? In what way have I wearied you?" (v. 3).

This is how the sixth chapter of Micah begins. Micah's community is watching cities fall around them and fearing an invasion themselves: the threat to safety, raid of their resources, destruction of their community. They are pleading to God to explain why they deserve such a state of being.

I feel like I can hear it—you know how in a crowd the shared energy of the group increases the intensity of the whole and everyone begins talking louder and faster and because the people to the right and the left of you are louder, you must get even louder . . . And then everyone is just screaming, "God, why are you doing this to us? Where are you?"

We know these questions, right? In response to impeachments and immigration, apathetic church folk and the challenges of navigating unloving systems, we ask, "God, where are you?"

And God offers a tender yet robust response: "I brought you from the land of Egypt and I redeemed you from slavery." For the people of Israel, this takes them all the way back to the beginning of their covenant with God when the Ten Commandments began by saying, "I am the LORD your God, who brought you out of the house of slavery; you shall have no other gods before me." *Oh.*

God continues, "I sent you Moses, Miriam, and Aaron—leaders with gifts and courage and joy to guide you." That list of names goes on to include Harriet Tubman and Oscar Romero, Tarana Burke and William Barber. *Yeah.*

"I transformed what was supposed to curse you into a blessing and protected you from the floods while you were crossing the sea." *Well.*

In each of these memories, the people of Israel recognize God's presence with them. They remember God's provision for them and hear again God's love toward them. They hear God asking, "How could any of these deeds have led you to these unjust ways of selfishness and evil?"

You can imagine the retreat, the silence, bowing of heads, softening of hearts. And in the disappointment they sense in God's voice, they remember how they have used power to take what was not theirs, allowed violence for the poor among them, and accepted leaders who lacked faithfulness. Our reality is not perfectly parallel, but we know the life of doubting God in the midst of being empowered and disempowered. God has done all these things for us, and what can we do to please God—should we bring a calf, a thousand rams, my firstborn son? Should I plan a revival, a churchwide fast, a new hashtag for next year?

The answer is no. God does not desire our routine liturgies of confession and our empty rituals of sacrifice. "Quit focusing on guidelines and hymnals"—this is God's message to the people of Israel and to us that lives spent on stale habits and formalities are not enough. God's acts of saving and redeeming are to encourage and inspire us to a freedom where we are no longer limited to religious practices but called to trusting relationship with God. To do this, God affirms who we are by reminding us of who God is.

If you dig deep into this passage, verses 6–8 are words of deliberation from the jury: this is not God speaking. When God spoke earlier, God used the pronoun *I*. These words come from the jury—the mountains and the hills. The passage personifies the mountains with capacity for judgment. The mountains refer to God as *he* and to the people as mortal. "He has told you, O mortal, what is good" (v. 8). Friends, the mountains are the witnesses to the goodness of God toward us! Forget your charges. Look beyond your narrow existence. Can't you see this? God has been good to you.

This goodness is the familiar word woven through Hebrew Scripture. After the sixth day of creating and all had been completed, Genesis 1:31 says that God saw everything that God had made and indeed, it was very good. The notion of goodness is a bedrock of Scripture and one of the most intriguing aspects of creation. The Hebrew word for "good" is *towb*. It means good, in the widest sense. Masculine and feminine, singular and plural—good is beautiful, best, joyful, pleasant, pleasureful, precious, ready. Because we are a part of this creation and this naming. We are good. We were made good.

The Twenty-Third Psalm that we all know well uses a form of *towb* in the word *goodness*. "You prepare a table before me in the presence of my enemies; you anoint my head with oil; my cup overflows. Surely goodness and mercy shall follow me all the days of my life" (vv. 5–6).

God is reminding the people of Israel: You know what is good. If you would just remember, you would not be wavering. If you would just remember, you would know that I am right here with you. If you would just remember, you could see my presence before you.

The witness of God's goodness flows on to us. Howard Thurman, in his book *Jesus and the Disinherited*, declares that Jesus was positioned divinely on the margins to encourage and uplift the most marginalized and oppressed among us. Thurman writes this text to "those who stand with their backs against the wall." Thurman says, "Wherever [Jesus'] spirit appears, the oppressed gather fresh courage; for God has announced the good news that fear, hypocrisy, and hatred, the three hounds of hell that track the trail of the disinherited, need have no dominion over them."[10]

I believe this is a message to remind us that God regularly shows up in mercy and blessing just where we least expect God to be—with the poor rather than the rich, with those who are mourning rather than celebrating, with the meek and the peacemakers rather than the strong and victorious. This is not where Micah's community or Jesus' listeners look for God, and if we are honest, we make this same mistake. If God shows up here, Jesus is saying, blessing the weak and the vulnerable, then God will be everywhere, showering all creation and its inhabitants with blessing.

THE WEARY SOUL REJOICES

God with us

The story of Jesus' birth is familiar and yet new every year. We know the events: an oppressive king and empire, the angel's blessing, Mary's yes, a sacred moment with Elizabeth, Zechariah's silence, Joseph's worry, a burdened journey, a baby who is God with us, and gifts from magi.

What makes this story new each year is our own resonance. These are not just elements of a story, or even parts of a story where we are reaching toward God. They are each enfleshed, meaning they engage the material parts of our lives—our bodies, our land, our culture, our experiences, our commitments. God comes to us within each of these parts of the Christmas narrative—in the familiarity and resonance of our lives and bodies. The pursuit of the story is whether we also risk embodiment.

Our encounter with the story of Jesus then requires that we identify with our own flesh to connect to this enfleshed story line. God comes to us as prophecy for gifts unseen, as courage in a birthing woman, as one who gives to our community as we anticipate change. How will we risk embodying the Divine?

DAY 25

Listen

Where refugees seek deliverance that never comes,
And the heart consumes itself, if it would live,
Where little children age before their time,
And life wears down the edges of the mind,
Where the old man sits with mind grown cold,
While bones and sinew, blood and cell, go slowly down to death,
Where fear companions each day's life,
And Perfect Love seems long delayed.
Christmas is waiting to be born:
In you, in me, in all of humankind.[11]

—Howard Thurman, "Christmas Is Waiting to Be Born"

i am free to wait . . .

For many, waiting is costly or painful. Some of our resistance to waiting stems from mere impatience. Some moments simply require that we wait. We are often waiting for a reason: what we are expecting likely improves our life conditions.

"Christmas Is Waiting to Be Born" lands as a voice of solidarity in this season of Advent, giving flesh to the agony of waiting. Howard Thurman wrote this piece in the realities of waiting and its connection to suffering.

What does it mean if we are Christmas?

Thurman's nuanced depiction of an old man growing cold gives attention to his suffering. We home in on the very meticulous reality of his blood and sinew. In the humanness of children losing their times of playfulness and optimism, this poem touches our own sorrow. And Thurman draws us into the quiet story of the human condition that lives in seasons of waiting that are indeed dark and lonely. We see suffering. We validate aching and pain. We are waiting for a Love we cannot yet see.

Thurman's line "where refugees seek deliverance that never comes" is an example of a people waiting with specific intention and deep need. The impact of waiting on our lives and the fading of the "edges of our mind" has real resonance on our resistance to waiting.

How do we become flesh for one another?

One of the most powerful characteristics of Thurman's writing and legacy is his simultaneous truth telling and faithfulness. Thurman rightfully holds many honored titles: pastor, mystic, scholar, especially in all the ways that he used these gifts to support the civil rights movement and Dr. Martin Luther King, Jr. Thurman's spirituality allowed him to hold an honest relationship with God that included personal darkness and social tragedies. As we find in this poem, he held the breadth of being human with the vision for what God also sees in us.

What are the ways that Perfect Love is born through us?

Christmas "being born" reminds us that it, too, is human. Christmas will linger in the belly of loving warmth even as it enters a cold but welcome embrace of life. Christmas will take on flesh, resonating with the human conditions it is born into. Our waiting is not ignored; it is met with new flesh—in you, in me, and in all of humankind.

What if these questions are the invitations in our waiting?

Breath prayer

Inhale: **The flesh of Christmas**

Exhale: **is my flesh.**

DAY 26

Listen

And Mary said,

"My soul magnifies the Lord,
    and my spirit rejoices in God my Savior,
for he has looked with favor on the lowly state of his servant.
    Surely from now on all generations will call me blessed,
for the Mighty One has done great things for me,
    and holy is his name;
indeed, his mercy is for those who fear him
    from generation to generation.
He has shown strength with his arm;
    he has scattered the proud in the imagination of their hearts.
He has brought down the powerful from their thrones
    and lifted up the lowly;
he has filled the hungry with good things
    and sent the rich away empty.
He has come to the aid of his child Israel,
    in remembrance of his mercy,
according to the promise he made to our ancestors,
    to Abraham and to his descendants forever."

–Luke 1:46-55

i am free to sing new truths.

The Song of Mary is the essence of Advent and the hope of Christmas.

As she sings these words, Mary is early in her awareness of her pregnancy and the ways that she is participating in the remaking of the world with God. As she is expecting, she is expectant with a faithfulness that imagines the world differently. With lyrics that anticipate the generational blessings she hasn't yet seen, Mary is a prophet.

Prophets tell stories that are grounded in the faith they know and a voice that speaks clearly of the present moment. With a lens to the Jewish stories of Mary's heart, this song echoes Miriam, Hannah, Judith, and Deborah. The women whose faith she witnessed in story and song are woven into her song of faith, and their legacy grounds her strength.

Central to her melody are the words *He has brought down the powerful from their thrones and lifted up the lowly; he has filled the hungry with good things and sent the rich away empty.* Without any sense of how this pregnancy or this vision will be realized, she imagines love and justice through this gift from God. Surrounded by the reality of oppression, Mary sings of a reordered world renewed by what God will bring forth.

Mary models the work of Advent in this song: accepting a season of waiting, welcoming God's presence in the journey, holding joy and the truths of her world, and imagining hope and justice being made known through her.

Today, her prophecy emerges from within her with its own voice. The coming and birth of Jesus is the definite and physical commitment of God to begin a turning around: a revolution. New, beautiful truth is born today. Like many new mothers who cling to their newborn and rejoice, I imagine Mary continues to sing. In the swaddled and infant body of Jesus, the face of power is new. She hums her lullaby through the night and for many years, preparing a path in his spirit—passing along the melodies of love and justice.

Within us, too, Advent has grown new hopes of what God will do. We've held them, wading through this season for a sign that the world is being prepared for more love and more justice. With hope wrapped in her arms, Mary invites us to sing of freedom with her today.

Breath prayer

Inhale: I sing today

Exhale: of the journey and the hope.

Listen

How beautiful upon the mountains
    are the feet of the messenger who announces peace,
who brings good news,
    who announces salvation,
    who says to Zion, "Your God reigns."
Listen! Your sentinels lift up their voices;
    together they shout for joy,
for in plain sight they see
    the return of the Lord to Zion.
Break forth; shout together for joy,
    you ruins of Jerusalem,
for the Lord has comforted his people;
    he has redeemed Jerusalem.
The Lord has bared his holy arm
    before the eyes of all the nations,
and all the ends of the earth shall see
    the salvation of our God.
                    —Isaiah 52:7-10

i am free to celebrate.

The feet of messengers is imagery that shows up frequently in the Bible, but here, the image of the mountain invites us to frame the news with specific grandeur. Physical messengers passed communication between homes and villages. We can imagine the hustle of a Christmas messenger as they excitingly traverse many terrains in varied weather. There's racing heartbeats, bated breath, and the opportunity to celebrate with each stop along the way. The passage situates the message "upon the mountains," associating the news with elevation and holiness. The breadth and importance of the birth of Jesus is itself a landscape, like that of a mountain, creating a backdrop or signpost by which many will now orient their lives. As with major events of our times, such as the beginning of the COVID-19 pandemic, important news shapes our timelines and perspectives.

We, too, can celebrate the presence of God with us, entering the world with both humanity and divinity. Verse 9 calls the reader to "break forth, shout for joy," expressing the excitement, endurance, and impact in the passage. And just as we do with the news of all babies, we appreciate its beauty in this moment and dream of its possibility in the days and years to come. What would it mean to imagine the same flurry in our own feet by moving in a spirit of celebration about what God is about to do in a big way?

The LORD has bared his holy arm before the eyes of all the nations.

God's arm is another familiar personification, sometimes referencing God's power and sometimes referring to the human agents that act with God. I wonder how these are the same in the body of Jesus and an invitation to those living into the joy of Christmas. God's arm references salvation, which provides an opportunity for people to enter relationship with God and learn of God's goodness. In all the ways that God's power will manifest, we again witness an enfleshed articulation of the work of God. And we are called as human agents to participate, with our bodies, with God's power.

The season and the intention of Christmas are not confined within this week or this season. We are feet and arms that also begin a celebration for the days ahead.

Breath prayer

Inhale: In my arms and feet,

Exhale: I feel the blessing of good news.

DAY 28

a prayer to be the Word

Italic text drawn from John 1:1–14.

In the beginning was the Word, and the Word was with God, and the Word was God. He was in the beginning with God. All things came into being through him, and without him not one thing came into being. What has come into being in him was life, and the life was the light of all people. The light shines in the darkness, and the darkness did not overtake it.

God of the beginning, your presence across time is beyond our imagination. And we confess that we only pretend to understand the essence of your Spirit in the world. But we know Truth and Wisdom and Love. We see it in the cypress tree, in grandmothers, and in moments of beautiful gift giving. Thank you for the ways you make the ordinary sacred, as it begins in you.

There was a man sent from God whose name was John. He came as a witness to testify to the light, so that all might believe through him. He himself was not the light, but he came to testify to the light. The true light, which enlightens everyone, was coming into the world.

He was in the world, and the world came into being through him, yet the world did not know him. He came to what was his own, and his own people did not accept him.

God who sent John, there are so many folks who claim to be Johns. Listening and looking for you is difficult. We desire to be witnesses, but the stage is crowded and foolish. In the dawn, can you help us notice the places of becoming?

But to all who received him, who believed in his name, he gave power to become children of God, who were born, not of blood or of the will of the flesh or of the will of man, but of God.

And the Word became flesh and lived among us, and we have seen his glory, the glory as of a father's only son, full of grace and truth.

God who became flesh, our bodies long for your grace and truth. Beyond our physical bodies, the communities and institutions that hold your name do not hold your power. Show us how to be flesh in those bodies, that your will might truly live among us. Make us your children, that we might bless generations with the Word you held in the beginning.

DAY 29

Listen

Grace to you and peace from God our Father and the Lord Jesus Christ.
I give thanks to my God always for you because of the grace of
God that has been given you in Christ Jesus, for in every way you
have been enriched in him, in speech and knowledge of every kind—
just as the testimony of Christ has been strengthened among you—
so that you are not lacking in any gift as you wait for the revealing of
our Lord Jesus Christ.

–1 Corinthians 1:3-7

i am free and grace-full.

I'm one of those people who is always running late. It's not usually because I
am unaware of time. I let myself get distracted—usually by other people—
and get delayed to my next destination. My children know this about me; it is
a running joke in our home, and they steal opportunities to announce this as
we arrive late to events. I do my best, however, to be punctual when it comes
to picking up our kids. I've failed many times.

In one instance, I was flying across town because I thought Wednesday
was Tuesday and soccer pickup time was violin pickup time and I arrived
thirty minutes late to get my youngest son. I was worried for him and mad
at myself. He was anxious and frustrated with me. He got in the car. We
breathed. I quickly said, "I'm sorry, son." He replied, "I am okay, Momma.
We are okay." And we both breathed again. His reply to me wasn't simply
forgiveness—he extended something more powerful back to me: grace.

The word *grace* has all kinds of meanings. Grace is sometimes the prayer of thanks we say over our meals. Grace is sometimes the extension of forgiveness we offer ourselves and others. In this scripture and all of Paul's letters, grace is used as a salutation and blessing to a community.

Grace to you and peace from God our Father and the Lord Jesus Christ. I give thanks to my God always for you because of the grace of God that has been given you in Christ Jesus. Paul is writing this letter to the church in Corinth with grace as his starting point. It is both a simple salutation and reverence to the power that is bigger than whatever human challenges he is planning to address. Rooted in the grace known through Jesus, a dynamic energy is produced—always moving and growing. This passage talks about grace as the source of enriching and strengthening our speech, knowledge, and testimony. I believe that grace is often the lifeblood that sustains families and communities. For my son and me that day, grace overcame the injury of my lateness. And it continues to overcome.

Some religious folks like to talk about cheap grace and costly grace— related to the sacrifices one has made to receive it. I don't believe that grace has a perfect or singular definition, nor do I think we need one. The abundance of understanding around grace is the most definitive.

Grace can show up in words across the modest parts of life, and it can emerge as a force that bridges conflict. Grace can be complex, joyous, simple, unearned, burdening, childlike, transactional, communal, and life-giving. In any experience of it, grace has a unique power within it. Like the words from my son, grace is an act of generosity offered from one heart to another.

Grace is a symbol of abundance for us as Christians. It becomes a bridge across conflict, doubt, and need. Like the Holy Spirit, it flows from God to us in a multiplicity of paths and forms. Against the message of scarcity or limitations, grace is present. Grace blesses. Grace extends. Grace abounds.

Breath prayer

Inhale: God offers grace,

Exhale: for all our needs.

DAY 30

SERMONETTE

Power to the People, Power in the People

In August of 1967, Dr. Martin Luther King Jr. delivered a presidential address at the annual convention of the Southern Christian Leadership Conference entitled "Where Do We Go from Here?" The body of this speech is significant, starting with an account of the organization's accomplishments in its first ten years. King celebrates Operation Bread Basket implemented nationally; voter registration drives in Grenada, Mississippi; successful demand for jobs in Cleveland, Ohio. And then from these accomplishments, he challenges the room of leaders: Where do we go from here? What's our next move? What matters now? These are familiar questions still.

In this SCLC address, King said,

Where do we go from here? First, we must massively assert our dignity and worth. We must stand amid a system that still oppresses us and develop a majestic set of values. We must no longer be ashamed of being black. Indeed, one of the greatest problems that the Negro confronts is his lack of power.

The Negro must rise up with an affirmation of his own Olympian manhood. The Negro will only be free when he reaches down to the inner depths of his own being and signs with the pen and ink of assertive manhood his own emancipation proclamation. As long as the mind is enslaved, the body can never be free.

And with a spirit straining toward true self-esteem, the Negro must boldly throw off the manacle of self-abnegation and say to

114

himself and to the world "I am somebody. I am a person. I am a man with dignity and honor. I have a rich and noble history, however painful and exploited that history has been. Yes, I was a slave through my foreparents and now I'm not ashamed of that. I'm ashamed of the people who were so sinful to make me a slave. We must stand up and say "I'm black but I'm black and beautiful."[12]

Power to the People. Power in the People. These are radical and sacred words that point to the foundation of how we create meaningful movement. Bold belief in Blackness. I repeat this invitation for those of us in the Black community and for those who seek to accompany us. Our collective discounting of Blackness has contributed to our current realities of oppression. This 1967 priority lingers as a gaping hole in the work of freedom for all Americans.

We talk power all the time—Fight the Power, Overcoming Powers, Power to the People. The memory of Dr. King invokes our commitment to engaging social powers. But this message of King drives in deeper—to our understandings of the power in Black bodies, Black communities, Black vitality. While our work still includes a reclamation of power to communities of need, the movement requires an intentional and inherent belief in value and beauty—one that cannot and does not come from anywhere else but emerges from within. Power to the people from somewhere else must happen, and our insistence on natural and intrinsic power in Blackness is also where we must go.

I believe that King spoke these words from his social consciousness and his desire to see Black people show up in the fullness of who we are. I also believe that King spoke these words as the Christ-following preacher that he was, longing for us to express the divinity within us. Living into our dignity and worth helps us take up the space that is ours in this world. And living into our dignity and worth is our right as creations of God. See, King was a scholar of the Word of God, and this appeal includes the spirit of other prophets. King echoes 1 John: "You are of God, little children, and have overcome them, because He who is in you is greater than he who is in the world" (1 John 4:4 NKJV).

This is uncomfortable to hold—imagining the fullness of your power or that of your neighbor. Power gets nasty. We struggle with it. Humility, abuses of power, trying to make sense of how we use the power we gain because of our education but still lacking it because of our race. King suggests that the problem is that love and power have usually been contrasted as opposites, so that love is connected to a resignation of power and power with a denial of love. To the SCLC, he asserted that Black Americans had sought their goals through love and moral suasion devoid of power, and white Americans had sought their goals through power devoid of love and conscience. Power at its best, he declared, is love implementing the demands of justice, and justice at its best is love correcting everything that stands against love.

To fully capture the context, this address was offered to the SCLC, an audience of predominantly Black and Christian leaders in the movement. King took this opportunity to speak directly into their experience and the mission of the organization. We know, though, that King's priorities consistently spanned the three oppressions of racism, materialism, and militarism. I believe his hope for the deep expressions of power from the Black community expanded to communities of poor people and many other communities affected by oppression. Additionally, King's passion extended to those who believe beyond the tradition of Christianity. The movement welcomes all who believe in the grand traditions of Love, Truth, and Justice.

There is deep connection between the theme I highlight of King and the actions going forth globally to amplify justice. I am certain: the bodies that march or know hunger or practice community in these ways do so because of their deep beliefs in their worth and the power of their identity. I am certain that the value of our bodies is informing the sacrifices being made so we can maintain the simple right to vote. They hold in their mind the ancestors who put their bodies on the line for privileges they did not get to enjoy. They look into the faces of our children—whose divine bodies and spirits we so deeply believe in. I am certain—the bold expressions of power we will see across our nation and world are rooted in the echo that King offers: I am somebody. I am a person with dignity and honor. I am Black or Brown or poor or trans or neurodivergent, and I have a rich story of hope to tell.

A NEW AND GLORIOUS MORN

Dawning in our spirits

Through Advent, we yearned for God and the holy in the night. Into Christmas, the holy was born in Christ and in us. This final week leads us into Epiphany, a season of light and revelation. The word *epiphany* comes from the Greek *epiphaneia*, meaning "appearing" or "revealing." According to all our songs and scriptures, light has valiantly returned and overcome the darkness that was our home in Advent.

I want to temper our tradition with the wisdom of creation and to consider the entry of light just as we transition from night to day. As our theme song reminds us, "a new and glorious morn" follows the dark night. In one quadrant of the sky, darkness lightens, a clearness begins to be seen. The edge where darkness and light meet slowly rises as a new day is revealed. In the same way, the entry of light into our lives is slow and staggered, miraculous and ordinary, beautiful and jarring. Yet the night is not forgotten or null as we bring its wisdom into the dawn of a new day.

DAY 31

Listen

"Here," she said, "in this here place, we flesh; flesh that weeps, laughs; flesh that dances bare feet in the grass. Love your flesh. Love it hard. Yonder they do not love our flesh. They despise it. They don't love your eyes; they'd just as soon pick em out. No more do they love the skin on your back. Yonder they flay it. And O my people they do not love your hands. Those they only use, tie, bind, chop off and leave empty. Love your hands! Love them. Raise them up and kiss them. Touch others with them, pat them together, stroke them on your face 'cause they don't love that either. You got to love it, *you!*"[13]

—Toni Morrison, *Beloved*

i am free to imagine the Christmas my body needs.

Beloved tells the story of emancipated and fugitive slaves seeking to build lives and families together amid their traumas and possibilities. From the genius of writer Toni Morrison, the book includes these lines from a sermon that character Baby Suggs delivers to her community in the spirit of hope and love. Baby Suggs personally knows the pain that members of this formerly enslaved community hold in their spirits and their bodies, and her words seek to restore them to wholeness.

Under the prophetic words of Baby Suggs, this sermon becomes a way to experience God. Women, men, and children gather in the clearing, a wide-open place cut out for gathering in the woods. They wait in the trees until her words and her staff draw them into the circle. These are words of ritual—to heal and to bless bodies that had been defiled and disconnected.

Suggs names each part of their body, calling it forth into life: eyes, hands, mouth, shoulders, arms, necks, feet, liver, lungs, and womb. Children given permission to laugh. Men released to dance while women weep for the living and the dead. In benediction, Suggs declares, "Love your heart," affirming the power of love and loving in their reconstructing lives.

The heart of Christmas is embodied. Christmas is a celebration of God being with us—coming to us in human form and joining our humanity. So many of the details of the Christmas narrative are disembodied and unaddressed. In our common narratives of Christmas, the holy family is white and is severed from the reality of the impacts of the Roman Empire on their bodies. We hide from the fear in their bodies as they travel toward Nazareth, and we don't give voice to the loneliness of birthing family outside of one's community.

All bodies will not relate to the embodiment and divinity of the Christmas narrative. The historical treatment of race, sex, and sexuality means that some bodies have been held up as the image of God while others have not. The traditional rituals of Christmas may focus our adoration on the baby of Jesus and his body, but these same practices may not help everyone see the work of God in their bodies.

For those whose bodies are marginalized, reread the blessing of Baby Suggs and hear the sacred blessing in her words, inviting God's inclusion into the bounty of Christmas.

Morrison captures the humanity of this formerly enslaved community and the ritual of freedom that summons them from darkness. Her blessing through Baby Suggs extends the imagination of this community to seeing themselves in the realm of blessing and wholeness. Like this response to slavocracy, rituals that respond to the unique healing of bodies so that they may be seen with divinity are another way that Christmas is made real.

Christmas does not come to us in one way or form. The expansiveness of our experiences and our bodies means that we use a wide range of language, images, and ritual to welcome the divinity that arrives in this season. It may look like lit candles and singing or tribal dancing in the woods, but Love is always present.

Breath prayer

Inhale: In this body,

Exhale: the Divine is also born.

DAY 32

Listen

When the time came for their purification according to the law of Moses, they brought him up to Jerusalem to present him to the Lord. . . .

Now there was a man in Jerusalem whose name was Simeon; this man was righteous and devout, looking forward to the consolation of Israel, and the Holy Spirit rested on him. It had been revealed to him by the Holy Spirit that he would not see death before he had seen the Lord's Messiah. Guided by the Spirit, Simeon came into the temple, and when the parents brought in the child Jesus to do for him what was customary under the law, Simeon took him in his arms and praised God, saying,

"Master, now you are dismissing your servant in peace,
    according to your word,
for my eyes have seen your salvation,
    which you have prepared in the presence of all peoples,
a light for revelation to the gentiles
    and for glory to your people Israel." . . .

There was also a prophet, Anna the daughter of Phanuel, of the tribe of Asher. She was of a great age, having lived with her husband seven years after her marriage, then as a widow to the age of eighty-four. She never left the temple but worshiped there with fasting and prayer night and day. At that moment she came and began to praise God and to speak about the child to all who were looking for the redemption of Jerusalem.

—Luke 2:22, 25-32, 36-38

i am free to struggle.

Dreams. Resolutions. Intentions.

None of these compare to the faith of Simeon and Anna.

After the verses about Jesus' birth, Luke places us in the temple with these two elders: Simeon, whom "the Holy Spirit rested upon" and who was told would not see death until he had seen the Lord's Messiah; and Anna, who had been widowed for decades, spending her life worshiping and fasting in the temple.

According to the passage, it was now forty days after Jesus' birth. His parents were again performing their duty as faithful Jews by returning to the temple, this time to offer a sacrifice and to consecrate their child to the Lord. They must have been in a reverent, even solemn mood that day, the way many young parents are when their first child is to be baptized. And so, for this very reason, they were perhaps startled, even frightened, when Simeon, old beyond years and beaming with ecstatic revelation, came up to them to touch the child and then began to sing. Simeon had waited for, prayed for, and sung about this day for many, many years, growing a faith that was being realized in this temple moment.

This is one of my favorite biblical passages to imagine visually—baby Jesus held in Anna's and Simeon's long-awaited and loving arms and encircled with their voices of celebration. Their movement is likely limited because of their frail and tired bodies. Yet the celebration of these two elders exudes from their mouths in melodies. Anna sings of thanksgiving, seeing a God who has kept promises in this new baby. Simeon's song is one of benediction: "You may now dismiss your servant in peace." He's not singing of angels and mangers but rather of letting go, of departing, of—truth be told—dying. In the infant Jesus, he has seen a sign and confirmation that the Lord has been faithful to the Israelites of old. Holding salvation in his arms, Simeon accepts his own death with completion.

The faith of these elders is textured and enduring in a way that I find rich and inspiring. I wonder if it is the lived experience of answered prayers or the stubborn patience they've grown to wait on God—or both. Waiting, doubting, seeing, questioning, expecting, mistrusting, hoping, struggling, moving forward in the dark, trusting—these are the practices of faith.

Depending on when you are reading this, today's reflection may fall on the seventh day of Kwanzaa, celebrating *imani,* or faith. In the African American tradition, *imani* represents the belief in the victory and righteousness of struggle. It is a day to acknowledge the struggles of life that have transformed into held beliefs. Anna and Simeon honor the *imani* of their lives in their temple songs. They invite those who are gathered and all of us who continue to imagine that day to see the presence of God and a victory of faith. Alongside the expectations of a new year, what are the ways you can look back and celebrate the struggles that have led to new beliefs?

Breath prayer

Inhale: I know the struggles of faith,

Exhale: and I celebrate them.

Listen

Samuel was ministering before the LORD, a boy wearing a linen ephod. His mother used to make for him a little robe and take it to him each year when she went up with her husband to offer the yearly sacrifice. Then Eli would bless Elkanah and his wife and say, "May the LORD repay you with children by this woman for the loan that she made to the LORD," and then they would return to their home....

Now the boy Samuel continued to grow both in stature and in favor with the LORD and with the people.

−1 Samuel 2:18-20, 26

i am free to hold the ordinary.

Christmas comes and goes quickly. By now, the glory of the season has likely faded and whatever material or spiritual beauty emerged has also now been met with the real edges of life. The birth of Jesus is an extraordinary story, expressed with humanity and divinity I cannot always relate to. Because I rarely see miracles like the Christmas story in my personal life, I sometimes look for the ordinary edges in a biblical story to help me relate.

I find what I'm looking for in the story of Hannah, Elkanah, and Samuel—another biblical narrative of a holy child that holds room for the ordinary. Hannah was barren and prayed for the gift of Samuel. A deep faithfulness grew from and in Samuel through Hannah's commitments and practices of faith. This passage includes a dedicated focus on the ephod: an apron-like piece of clothing Hannah would make for Samuel each year that mimicked the clothing of the priest. Because she held her son as a gift from God, Hannah was in a rhythm of preparing this garment that would draw her son back into the presence of God.

I imagine the days where Hannah sat with the needle and thread in her hand and a pile of linen in her lap. My imagination includes her sitting in a circle with other Jewish women preparing garments and enjoying the fellowship of one another. They have known together the seasons of waiting and the joys of arrival. So sewn into the fabric is also the gratitude and wisdom of community, their collective hopes for what God might do with what they can make in their hands and in their hearts. Hannah's care for this garment is held in the suffering that preceded the gift of Samuel and her presence to his ongoing care.

Whatever we have carried out of the Advent season is a gift that deserves this same care: the honesty and wisdom of how we practically care for it. Though contextually different, Hannah's pattern gives us a guide for how we can hold the sacred gifts of our lives. In the making of the ephod, we gather with people who have witnessed our journey and give us space to make new hope. In the way Hannah clothed Samuel, we commit to clothe our gifts in the best that our hopes can imagine. In the practice of the yearly sacrifice, we keep going to the places where we know we've met God before, presenting our gifts of hope again and again.

In this season, we pay attention to the gifts of children in Jesus and Samuel. Gifts in boxes have come our way, and the season of Advent has offered gifts for our spirits. What do we do with extraordinary gifts in our ordinary hands?

Breath prayer

Inhale: In my ordinary hands,

Exhale: I care for the sacred.

DAY 34

a prayer for wisdom

Text in roman font is from Sirach 24:1–7.

Wisdom praises herself
    and tells of her glory in the midst of her people.

God who is Wisdom, you are new, but I have known you. You are God. And you are Wisdom. And you are she. I've felt your breath and known the comfort of your presence when I was afraid. There is so much I want to learn from you. Your coming to live among us, to be with us, is like the slow rising of the sun. Remind me of the comfort held within you. Tell me of your glory.

In the assembly of the Most High she opens her mouth,
    and in the presence of his hosts she tells of her glory:
"I came forth from the mouth of the Most High
    and covered the earth like a mist.
I encamped in the heights,
    and my throne was in a pillar of cloud."

Wisdom who is glory, your essence flows through silence and darkness and remains as light and sound emerge. Wisdom comes forth, covers, and encamps. Your presence surrounds all of creation. I confess that sometimes your nature is too big to discern. And because wisdom is sometimes beyond logic and rationale, I ignore you and depend on what I know. Help me to stop reducing all knowing to what I can understand. Protect me from the lie that your work is always nebulous or confusing. Show me how to notice and listen for your glory.

> "Alone I compassed the vault of heaven
>> and traversed the depths of the abyss.
> Over waves of the sea, over all the earth,
>> and over every people and nation I have held sway.
> Among all these I sought a resting place;
>> in whose inheritance should I abide?"

Wisdom who abides, as we conclude these seasons, stay with us. Let us hold the tension of darkness that persists as we trust the ways you encompass the abysses of our lives. Give me the courage of Mary, mother of Jesus, who sang of your glory as you appeared. In the rivers and the fields, let me find you. In the children and the elders, let me see you. In you, Wisdom, I receive the Holy Spirit within me and welcome the glory that lives in my spirit.

Bless my knowing and unknowing, and for generations to come, abide with us.

DAY 35

Listen

Arise, shine, for your light has come,
    and the glory of the LORD has risen upon you.
For darkness shall cover the earth
    and thick darkness the peoples,
but the LORD will arise upon you,
    and his glory will appear over you. . . .

Lift up your eyes and look around;
    they all gather together; they come to you;
your sons shall come from far away,
    and your daughters shall be carried in their nurses' arms.
Then you shall see and be radiant;
    your heart shall thrill and rejoice,
because the abundance of the sea shall be brought to you;
    the wealth of the nations shall come to you.

                –Isaiah 60:1-2, 4-5

i am free to look for Light.

At its simplest level, Epiphany provides the last scene of the Christmas story. The magi in the story come from the east as the first visitors to celebrate and acknowledge the significance of the birth of Jesus. On the journey, the magi take their guidance from a star in the sky, pointing them to Bethlehem as they ride through the days and nights.

On the feast of Epiphany, we celebrate the arrival of the sages from afar to the manger in Bethlehem where the infant Jesus lies swaddled. He is surrounded by animals, watched over by parents, and illumined by an amazing star. Epiphany falls on the twelfth day after Christmas, closing one season of the church year and opening another.

In the Greek language, the word *epiphany* means to reveal or appear. The call of the prophet Isaiah points toward a moment that cannot yet be seen but can be longed for. The demands of darkness and the expectancy of light are felt. This passage is spoken to encourage a dispirited people to see God's transformative light coming just over the horizon and to imagine that when that light breaks over Zion, the glory of God will be revealed to them and in them.

This text is tough; we feel the tension of the hope and absence of light, even as we know it does come. This is an honest tension, honoring the gifts that we know live in the darkness and the welcome light revealed through Christ. The story of Christmas assumes a radiant fullness of light and power in all places for all people. Realistically, Christmas and the new year have come, but there hasn't been much space for us to see what will actually be born from the darkness of Advent and the hope of Christ.

The Light that comes to us in Epiphany will mean many things in the same rhythmic cycle that we know as day and night. Jesus will bring God's light into the world as embodiment of God, but will also bring divinity to our humanity. The light of Epiphany holds hope for the power of God to break through the increasing despair among us with abundant love. The light of Epiphany introduces a reclamation of authority, expanding the giving of gifts beyond the kingdom.

Lift up your eyes and look around.

Light is emerging slowly—as a baby grows and power breaks through and spaces are reclaimed. It is not rapid or complete, but it is natural. As Isaiah directs our eyes, we see the breaking in of light in the ordinary places like the movement of children and the abundance of the seas. In your waiting and in the dark, "lift up and look around," says Isaiah in this passage. In the mountains and the waters that surround us, the Light is infused, and power will break through. In the shouts of joy from the elders and the squeals of delight from children, there is our recentering.

Breath prayer

Inhale: I know Light is coming.

Exhale: I don't have to worry.

DAY 36

Listen

For the love of Christ urges us on, because we are convinced that one has died for all; therefore all have died. And he died for all, so that those who live might live no longer for themselves but for the one who for their sake died and was raised.

From now on, therefore, we regard no one from a human point of view; even though we once knew Christ from a human point of view, we no longer know him in that way. So if anyone is in Christ, there is a new creation: everything old has passed away; look, new things have come into being!

—2 Corinthians 5:14-17

SERMONETTE

Love Dawning

Picture it: The city of Corinth, about 55 CE. Geographically, Corinth was perched on a small piece of land surrounded by water, and travel to places like Athens or Sparta had to pass through Corinthian land. People referred to it as the bridge of Greece. For centuries, this was the hub of commercial life in the Mediterranean world. Trade flourished by land and by sea. From Italy and the Iberian Peninsula, goods flowed through large harbors and from smaller ships from Phoenicia and Egypt. Wool, spices, wine, horses, wives—all this was passing between hands.

There were more than twelve temples in Corinth. In addition to a Jewish synagogue, a temple to Aphrodite, the goddess of love, another to the god of healing, another to Apollo. Greek culture boomed. It wasn't an educational center like Athens, but philosophies and wisdom were of great value. Visualize all the people and language and cultures that flowed through Corinth. Imagine the tension and speed of ideas and ethics. The phrase "to live like a Corinthian" meant to live in wealth and luxury, drunkenness, and questionable ethics.

When I imagine the sociological reality of Corinth, it feels very much like Facebook. All these people with varying ideas and freedoms and backgrounds converging in a space with a constant buzz of commercialism in the background. Paul writes his letters to people who are burdened with the work of being community in the midst of this. Our scripture comes from 2 Corinthians, a reattempt to offer guidance to the leaders of this body toward unity and understanding around the work and blessing of Christ.

These words were written to a people who, like us, lived in a culture with strong influence and appeal to be in competition and have power, to be better and more right than one another—forsaking one's nature for participation in the culture. The New Jerusalem Bible offers our scripture with these words:

> The love of Christ overwhelms us whenever we reflect on this: that if one person has died for all, then all have died. The reason Christ died for all was so that the living should live no longer for themselves, but for Christ.

The love of Christ overwhelms us. Have you ever been overwhelmed? Like, for real? The very nature of being overwhelmed means that what was important has been forced aside for a new priority. The love of Christ has done this. With his birth, it has overwhelmed every need that was separating us from him. His capacity to be so vulnerable overwhelms any way we might look good. His provision for our souls overwhelms our knowing. His willingness to die overwhelms our sense of control. His resurrection overwhelms our rightness. The presence of Jesus means that we are invited into a love that has enough power to overwhelm the needs to which we are so wedded. Our participation in that love calls us to let it become our new priority—to let those needs be overwhelmed, pushed aside, washed away. Our relationship with Christ invites us to center his love, redefining our needs.

I recently listened to a 2017 episode of *Fresh Air* on NPR where Terry Gross interviewed an editor and lexicographer for Merriam-Webster. Kory Stamper's job was to identify new words to be added to the dictionary each year. For 2017, *binge-watch* and *photobomb* and *humblebrag* were new additions to the dictionary. (Go google them!)

Stamper talked about the process of adding new words and the criteria they use. I'd never really given it that much thought, but she explained how the first step is to pay attention to widespread use—how new words are being used across different mediums and contexts. The second criteria is shelf life. Has the use of the word been sustained? Another criteria is whether the word has actual meaning. Stamper went on to say that the process is not about policing the language, it is about noticing changes in the ways we use language so that new words can be added or the meaning of old words can be modified.

I was struck by her words. To think of new words in the dictionary, I imagined some overwhelming process of having to invent or produce or generate something from raw materials. She used the verbs *notice*, *add*, and *modify*. In the same ways that words and language are formed, can creation be the work of noticing and adding and modifying? Could loving in a Christlike way be the practice of noticing, adding, and modifying?

For many of us, creativity is heavy work, and the ability to see anything new is distant. Our imaginations are impoverished and atrophied. For some of us it's hardest to notice God in others, for some of us it's hardest to notice God in ourselves. We are reminded that love creates. Because love is among us, so is the breaking in of something new.

New creation, however, is conceived in imagination . . . and imagination begins in prayer, in the images that God plants in us. Prayer, of course, begins in holy silence. When we let ourselves slow down and begin to listen for the subtle movements in our hearts and spirits, then we can begin to feel the pull of love and hear the call of new creation. It is then that we stop seeing from a human point of view and begin to see with new eyes of Christ.

Everything new starts in the dark. In wombs, in soil, in the dawn of Sunday mornings, in imaginations, in prayer. To find love or space to imagine it, we can always start by simply closing our eyes.

A PRAYER FOR THIS SEASON AND THE NEXT

There is holy.
Holy that created and grounded all things in Love.
Holy that makes space for fellowship in rituals and memories.
Holy that calls us out of the chaos and into peace.
Holy that invites us into dark places to see anew.
God who is holy, remind us that we are made in Love and that your
    love is always calling us into freedom.

There is holy in the night.
Holy in my fears,
holy in my questions,
holy in my struggles.
Holy in the soil.
God who fills the night, give me the freedom to reclaim your divine
    work in the dark places of my life.

The Holy in the Night

The holy reaches into the night.
Beyond our oppressive systems to empower the margins,
nudging our complacent hearts to release truth and hope,
to the places where justice for people and land is yet undone,
where our most divine dreams lie dormant.
God who knows longing, move our spirits and our bodies toward
    holy ground.

Holy comes in bodies.
In pregnant bodies expanding with faithful courage,
in vulnerable babies who share the face of God,
in the wisdom of our own flesh,
in the communities of solidarity we make together.
God who lives in the womb of the people, be with us.

Out of the holy in the night, the Divine is revealed.
Expressed in our knowing and our wisdom,
a story of hope unfolding,
with Love recentered and calling us to new postures,
witnessed in the dawning of every morning,
there is holy in the night. From this holy, Light is born.

SMALL GROUP GUIDE

I believe my ancestors knew things about freedom I can't even begin to articulate myself. Maybe liberation is not as linear as we assume. Each generation may seem more liberated, but there are always new forms of bondage. It is much better, then, to learn what freedom sounds like. Just because you've found it once doesn't mean you will never wander again. We must teach our children and our children's children what it means to be free. What it feels like to be whole. To exhale. And stories are our greatest teachers.[14]
    –Cole Arthur Riley, *This Here Flesh*

We practice freedom in community. The important gleanings from our individual reflections get celebrated and refined as we connect them with others who are committed to the same. This section offers six guides to sharing this study together in family or faith community settings. The guides match the six devotional themes and could be used for repeated gatherings that mark the traditional six weeks of Advent, Christmas, and Epiphany. Each session invites the group to share stories in response to the daily reflections. In the spirit of Cole Arthur Riley's wisdom, this guide leans into weekly spaces that highlight the sounds of freedom with song and poetry to affirm the storytelling of the group.

GATHERING 1

O Holy Night: The Possibility of Freedom

SHARING SCRIPTURE: PSALM 145

SHARING ART

> Call it
> the waters of salvation
> or the garlands of gladness.
>
> Call it
> the grave-clothes
> falling away
> or call it the loosing
> of the chains.
>
> Call it
> what binds us together:
> fierce but
> fragile but
> fierce.
>
> Call it
> *he will rejoice over you*
> *with gladness;*
> call it
> *he will renew you*

in his love;
call it
he will exult over you
with loud singing
as on a day
of festival.

Call it
the thin, thin place
where the veil
gives way.

Or call it this:
the path we make
when we go deep
and deeper still
into the dark
and look behind to see
the way has been lit
by our rejoicing.[15]
    —Jan Richardson, "As on a Day of Festival"

SHARING STORY

Think of how the story of Noah drew on the shared history of the original Jewish audience to remind them of God's faithfulness. What are stories from your history or family history that remind you of blessings in the midst of not knowing? Explore the language of possibilities and share ways you have been drawn into new possibilities.

SHARING PRAYER

Leader: God of deep and dazzling darkness,
          here on the edge of night
          before we surrender our day
          to silence and mystery,
          we need to hear that you love us.

People: **We need to hear again your promise never to leave us;
          we need to hope in you.**

Leader: Hear our prayer for all who weep tonight,
          and those who wait beside the dying. (*pause . . .*)
          Hear our prayer for frightened children,
          for anxious parents and families in distress. (*pause . . .*)
          Hear our prayer for nations at war,
          for hungry refugees and those unjustly oppressed. (*pause . . .*)
          Hear all our prayers

All: *God of deep and dazzling darkness,
     our world is in your hands,
     and so are we.
     We rest in you.
     In Jesus' name. Amen.*[16]

–Marlene Kropf, in *Sing the Story*

SERMON REFLECTIONS (CONTINUED FROM DAY 6)

Job and Job's Wife: Making Sense of Darkness (Job 2:7-10)

The book of Job is hard. It's complex and unsettling, raising more questions than it answers. Job allows us to wrestle with the question of suffering and how it relates to the presence of our faith. Why is there suffering? How is our faith related to our blessings? How do we navigate our faith when there is more suffering than blessing?

In the first chapter of Job, we witness the death of his children and servants, as well as the loss of his home and property (Job 1:13–19). In response to these realities, Job responds, "Naked I came from my mother's womb, and naked shall I return there; the LORD gave, and the LORD has taken away; blessed be the name of the LORD" (1:21). Our biblical history reminds us that children and property not only represented one's worth. They served as currency: the way one negotiated business and relationships for livelihood. Children and property also represented legacy: how health and wealth continued beyond one's life. Despite these tragic realities, as well as Job's ensuing questions and despair, we hear Job's commitment to God. More than many other biblical stories, with Job's narrative we linger in a longing for God's healing amid faithfulness and suffering.

Our theological conversations around Job often focus on the literal loss of his possessions, the magnitude of "things" he lost. With our own capacity to understand the relationship between economic, social, and emotional losses, we can also imagine the reality of Job's situation. Surely Job carried grief as he negotiated living without these things he once had. We don't hear these in the biblical narrative, but anger, anxiety, and guilt are other natural responses to such loss.

Questioning and doubt have consistently lived in tension with faith. The question from Job's wife seems to automatically live in opposition to faith. Religion and theology sometimes have taught us that when we question or hold doubt, we are not practicing the faith to which God has called us. However, Richard Rohr, a Franciscan priest and spiritual writer, suggests, "The opposite of faith is not doubt; the opposite of faith is control. You must leave the Garden, where there are angels with flaming swords to keep you from ever really returning. You must leave the womb to be born."[17] For Rohr, faith and doubt are correlative terms, working together toward life with God. Rohr understands and suggests faith as a way of being that draws us into what Job's wife does: she engages a "spirit of questing, a desire for understanding."[18]

Mother Teresa is celebrated for having a type of faithfulness that inspires, and it endured through deep compassion. Through her private writings, we learn that her relationship with God knew much doubt and isolation, and her prayer life held great darkness. Her writings named the many unanswered questions she held of God and even wavered into questioning the presence of God. But her questions do not discount her depth of faithfulness. Mother Teresa models for us that even saints have doubts. Can we extend this same understanding toward the wife of Job?

Wrestling with God

A study note in *The CEB Women's Bible* offers another nuanced perspective on Job's wife:

> Could Mrs. Job have been offering her husband a way to handle his grief? A life of prosperity often excludes the need to wrestle with God, to seek fervently the divine will, and to cry out in protest and in pain against God. In her anger, Mrs. Job potentially empowers her husband to seek a deeper, more authentic understanding of God in the midst of his struggle.[19]

Job's own response to God did include struggle and has been the subject of much biblical scholarship that is far beyond the scope of this study. Still, although Job's faith was not always certain (see Job 30:20–31), it is a contrast to the authentic doubts expressed by his wife. However, as we witness the responses of both Job and his wife as crucial components of faith, the book of Job will continue to be an invitation toward faithfulness. I wonder if we might allow ourselves to experience the faith of his wife as an invitation or model to be with God in a different yet valuable way. Even with his questions, Job was persevering, determined, righteous. Job's wife was questioning, doubtful, and authentic. Despite their stark differences, these two responses communicate faithful paths toward relationship and healing with God. In them, we hear genuine longing for God's healing.

As we consider the question of healing or wholeness in the context of this couple's faithfulness, we are invited to consider our own understandings of how we can come to God. Every trial we encounter will not allow us to turn toward God with the determination of Job. Sometimes we come with real doubts, yet this does not prevent our access to healing and wholeness through God. Questions and doubt are viable paths toward God when we offer them in faith. Although I am comparing the faith of Job with the more doubtful faith of his wife, I am not pitting them in competition with each other. Their responses are equally valid and necessarily different.

Our culture is often caught in cycles of glorifying logic and certainty. We do this in a way that diminishes intuition or other ways of non-logical knowing. The narrative of Job's wife celebrates other paths of reaching toward God's healing. Rohr says, "Rational certitude is exactly what the Scriptures do not offer us. They offer us something much better and an entirely different way of knowing: an intimate relationship, a dark journey, a path where we must discover for ourselves that grace, love, mercy and forgiveness are absolutely necessary for survival in an uncertain world."[20] These emerge as Job and Job's wife make sense of darkness in different ways, seeing the possibilities that practices of faith and practices of doubt offer their needs.

GATHERING 2

The Stars Are Brightly Shining: Tools for the Night

SHARING SCRIPTURE: PHILIPPIANS 1:3-11

SHARING ART

Depending on your location, use this art space to be tactile with parts of nature. Gather seeds, leaves, snow, or rocks and use a few minutes to hold them in your hands. As you acknowledge their journeys through days and seasons, pay attention to the ways they move between temperatures, climate, and daylight.

SHARING STORY

The reflections for Days 7–12 include invitations to tools that help us navigate the darkness: considering legacy, repentance, remembering the waters of baptism, understanding preparation in pieces, questioning, and others. Which of these practices helped you make sense of the dark? Were there practices that complicated your experience of darkness? Did any of these practices help you find trust or comfort with darkness?

SHARING PRAYER

Use these breath prayers to remind yourself of the wisdom in familiar scriptures:

Inhale: It is well	*Exhale:* with my soul.
Inhale: God is	*Exhale:* my strength and song.
Inhale: Guide my feet,	*Exhale:* while I run this race.
Inhale: Not my will,	*Exhale:* let your will be done.
Inhale: Be still,	*Exhale:* and know that I am God.

SERMON REFLECTIONS (CONTINUED FROM DAY 12)

Oil and Grace, Tools for Our Faith (John 12:1-8)

Just as in the story of the prodigal son and his brother, there are differences and tensions in how we come broken but seeking healing. We should be careful, too, about how we polarize Mary and Judas in this passage. The reality is that they both take uncomfortable and complicated risks, with differing levels of discernment. In any other moment, Mary's actions might have been perceived as discreditable instead of prophetic, and Judas's words could be sound stewardship advice instead of selfish discomfort.

The power of our mistakes to define us finds resistance in the presence of grace. Shame is dialed backed to the actual things we did wrong, and we can truthfully hold them up to receive the mercy and anointing of Christ.

One story of shame might say: *I made the mistake of not working as hard as I am capable of in school. The shame I carry of being called lazy and unsuccessful cannot linger. That is not who I am and will not be the funk that becomes me. I receive the sweet-smelling forgiveness of Christ, and I am worthy of respect and integrity, called to live into my potential.*

Another story would be: *We are Christians in a country that privileges our beliefs. We regularly take for granted the freedoms we enjoy because of this and ignore the challenges of people without our privilege. Recognizing this imbalance of power, our faith is not corrupt, nor are we bad believers. We accept the forgiveness of Christ, releasing us from the burden of this shame, and accept the responsibility of the power and identities we hold.*

It is while we smell death that we can smell life. It is while we smell a rotting body in a tomb that we can smell the earth underneath the stone as it is being rolled away. It is while we can barely stand the smell of Lazarus that Mary pours perfume on Jesus' feet. This is the power of smell—permeating our life with the good and the bad, the powerful and the painful. Our relationship with God and our most genuine acts of faith include the blend of these scents.

GATHERING 3

It Is the Night: Dwelling in the Truth

SHARING SCRIPTURE: PSALM 91:9-16

SHARING ART

With paper and writing utensils, take three minutes to freewrite, releasing as many filters as possible. What people, places, or moments emerge from the following words: *home, abide, loved, heard, protected?*

SHARING STORY

Dwelling, in the invitation of the reflections for Days 13–18, is a familiar practice. We dwell in places that are welcoming and comfortable, often making those places our homes. Where are the places you have dwelled? How do the characteristics of those places compare to this season of Advent for you?

SHARING PRAYER

> Sing and sing. And when you cannot raise a note of song,
>
> the rocks will cry out. And when the echoing stones go still,
> in the dangerous crevice that is your heart, if you lie still,
>
> there remains an altar, a way to enter
> a terrible holiness, a lush and delicate calm.[21]
> > **—David Wright, in *A Liturgy for Stones***

SERMON REFLECTIONS (CONTINUED FROM DAY 18)

Confession as a Dwelling Practice (1 John 1:1-3, 8-9)

First John is often referred to as the love letter of the Bible because it celebrates and honors that the love of God in consistent and beautiful ways. This book is where we get the profound declaration that "God is love." The writer of 1 John wrote this letter to set the record straight, so to speak, about these matters, probably with the fear that current members of the community might split off to join the dissenters. Confession is a practice toward the gift of relationship.

The New Testament is always calling us to do what we cannot do—to love our enemies, to bless those who persecute us, to pray without ceasing, to be perfect as God in heaven is perfect. The New Testament commands us to live these impossibilities because what is impossible with human beings is possible with God; because we are promised that as we put one foot in front of the other to seek to live out these commands, what is commanded of us is given as a gift. No, we ourselves cannot forgive, but as we strive to forgive, we are given God's forgiveness as a gift.

We are not called to create forgiveness; that is beyond us. We are called instead to participate in a forgiveness given to us as a gift. All our efforts to forgive those who have hurt and wronged us, efforts that are broken, partial, incomplete, and stained, are gathered into the forgiveness that is full, whole, and pure—the forgiveness that God gives in Jesus Christ.

In our struggle through the hurts and pains of life, we must cling with all our heart to God's hope in forgiveness. Real forgiveness is available to all people—a forgiveness that satisfies our deepest longing to be cleansed inside and out. Through Christ, all our sins have been forgiven. God's plan is that our confession would return our heart to God. God desires that we turn from that sin, ask forgiveness—both from God and from those we hurt—make reparation when possible, and then walk on with God. We must let go of that sin, leaving no regret behind as we continue on with our Lord.

No wonder almost two-thirds of Jesus' teaching is directly or indirectly about forgiveness. The ways we relate together include taking sides, bitterness, holding grudges, and violence. We all need to apologize, and we all need to forgive. Otherwise, we are controlled by the past, individually and corporately. Only mutual apology, healing, and forgiveness offer a sustainable future for humanity.

GATHERING 4

In Sin and Error Pining: Longing for a Savior

SHARING SCRIPTURE: PSALM 126

SHARING ART

Listen to or read the lyrics of "Someday at Christmas" by Stevie Wonder.

SHARING STORY

Our proximity to the good news exposes the bad, and this week holds the burden of facing truths and bad news. What parts of the truth or other burdens are you wrestling with? How do you see the work of Christmas transforming it?

SHARING PRAYER

> To look on God's face
> To dwell within the gaze
>   of a destitute child
> To see in his eyes flecks of light
>   that will shatter darkness
> To stand in the slight presence
>   that will tear the world asunder
> To bear witness to the ageless story of hope
>   just now in infancy
> To find footing along the path of salvation
>   being unfurled, flung far and wide
> To hear the mighty voice of God in whisper
> and to know:
> *Now it begins.*[22]
>
> **–George Dupuy, in *Sing the Story***

SERMON REFLECTIONS *(CONTINUED FROM DAY 24)*

God's Hope for the Future (Micah 6:8; Matthew 5:3-12)

In Matthew 5, we are still perched on the mountain of God's goodness as the Sermon on the Mount begins. I have always loved the visual of how the Sermon on the Mount starts. The very first verse of chapter 5 says that Jesus saw the crowds, went up to the mountain, sat down, and the disciples came to him. The scene is laden with the importance and value of what he is to impart. I envision Jesus seeing these people and knowing he had a daunting task before him. He sits, as a rabbi would do in his day, and allows the gospel to unfold.

The Beatitudes, much like the Micah passage, have an essence that has been embedded within us. But I am going to confess: for most of my hearing of this passage, I believe I was deceived by the Beatitudes, even coining the term "Beatitudes deception." I'll guess that I'm not alone. Hearing and being taught the Beatitudes, it is hard for me to not hear Jesus setting up terms in which I might be blessed.

This deception is as simple as it is subtle: believing that Jesus is setting up the conditions of blessing, rather than actually blessing his hearers. For instance, when I hear "Blessed are the poor in spirit, for theirs is the kingdom of heaven," I tend to think, "Am I poor enough in spirit?" or "I should try to be poorer in spirit." Or, when I hear "Blessed are the peacemakers . . . ," I think, "Yes, I really should be more committed to making peace." In reading the Beatitudes, I could not focus on the blessing, because I was focused on what felt like deficiencies.

Listening more closely to the words of this passage, it is helpful to recall that though the New Testament is written in Greek, when Jesus sat down to offer the Sermon on the Mount, he began to speak the Beatitudes in Aramaic, a form of Hebrew spoken in his day. In the Aramaic language, there is no word for "are." This word gets added to our English translations. This means that there is no verb in the original sentences, there is no *are*. We hear them as proclamations: "Blessed are the meek," but Jesus spoke them more as exclamations: "O the blessedness of the meek!" Complete game-changer. Deception uncovered.

The Beatitudes were not spoken as pious hopes of what shall be; they are not glowing prophecies of some future bliss—they are declarations of what is. In the words "O the blessedness of the persecuted," the blessedness of Christians is not postponed to some future glory. It is one that exists here and now. And what I had been hearing as a blessing only for those who could live up to these virtuous standards actually erases all the walls I had built and knocks me over the head with a blessing that is already mine. And the love and affirmation I expected to walk into once I reached these places now suddenly surrounds me.

Speaking in Aramaic offers another layer of blessing. Using this dialect and formatting, each phrase in this blessed-for pattern would have reminded the listeners of the Psalms. The first chapter and first verse of Psalms says, "O the blessedness of those who do not follow the wicked." Much like someone putting new words on your favorite hymn, the crowds gathered for the sermon would have heard the rhythm and tongue of the Beatitudes and would have instantly recognized something very familiar and wonderfully larger than that moment.

For each of us, there is a voice, a sound, a song that places us in a space of deep familiarity. For me, it's my grandaddy singing "I Need Thee Every Hour." And that is the tone that Jesus is using, part of the message that Jesus is teaching, prompting the memories of our ears and hearts. Whether we have forsaken God, whether we are feeling like God has forsaken us, whether we are poor in spirit, mourning, meek . . . God is saying, "I have been here with you, I am here, and I am still blessing you."

GATHERING 5

The Weary Soul Rejoices: God with Us

SHARING SCRIPTURE: ISAIAH 9:2-7

SHARING ART

At the Impulse of God's Love: A Re-envisioning of Dirk Willems Saving His Captor's Life (1685) by Jan Luykens, Michelle L. Hofer. Used with permission.

SHARING STORY

Including ourselves, especially our bodies, has likely been uncomfortable for many. There is long history and deep impact of removing talk and awareness of our bodies in church and theology. Share about some of the experiences that people hold around their bodies being included or excluded in our practices of faith.

SHARING PRAYER

Use the diverse abilities and capacities in your group and use your bodies to make rhythmic sounds together. By clapping, humming, tapping feet, using objects as drums, and so on, coordinate the movements of your bodies in shared rhythm. Make a few minutes of music together.

SERMON REFLECTIONS (CONTINUED FROM DAY 30)

Power to the People, Power in the People

We can hear King repeating Paul's words to the church in Ephesians: "I also pray that you understand the incredible greatness of God's power for us who believe him. This is the same mighty power that raised Christ from the dead" (Ephesians 1:19–20 NLT). We also hear the words to the Romans: "The Spirit of God, who raised Jesus from the dead, lives in you. And just as God raised Christ Jesus from the dead, he will give life to your mortal bodies by this same Spirit living within you" (Romans 8:11 NLT).

In the 2022 commemoration of Martin Luther King Jr. Day, Dr. Bernice King and the King Center entitled the call to shift priorities to the interconnected relationships that compose beloved community "It Starts with Me"—seeing all of creation as integral and centering our values from things to people, from the artificial to the authentic. If you've been tapped in, you know that central to the message from the King Center is also our imperative attention to voting rights legislation as it makes its way through the US Congress. Leaders are marching in Washington across the Frederick Douglass Memorial Bridge, and there is a group into their third day of a hunger strike. The honoring of this message starts with what we do in and with our own bodies.

GATHERING 6

A New and Glorious Morn: Dawning in Our Spirits

SHARING SCRIPTURE: COLOSSIANS 3:12-17

SHARING ART

In your gathering space, ask permission to experiment with shades of light and darkness. Adjust your room lighting, offer a candle, change your seating for more or less exposure to exterior windows and doors. Pay attention to your sense of light and darkness in the space where you are gathered.

SHARING STORY

This final week highlights our shift from darkness to light. How are you noticing that transition in your own life and spirit? Have you noticed any changes in your relationship with darkness? What are expressions of Light you want to share and celebrate?

SHARING PRAYER

Leader: From where we are
to where you need us,

All: Jesus, now lead on.

Leader: From the security of what we know
to the adventure of what you will reveal,

All: Jesus, now lead on.

Leader: To refashion the fabric of this world
until it resembles the shape of your kingdom,

All: Jesus, now lead on.

Leader: Because good things have been prepared
for those who love God,

All: *Jesus, now lead on.* [23]

> —Iona Community, *Stages on the Way*

SERMON REFLECTIONS (CONTINUED FROM DAY 36)

Love Dawning (2 Corinthians 5:14-17)

This is a recentering. This is a new world. We are in new relationship. Paul says: "And for anyone who is in Christ, there is a new creation." This is a familiar passage. The older versions, the ones stuck in our memory, remind us, "If anyone is in Christ, there is a new creation." It's an if-then conditional statement: *If* a certain condition is true, *then* a particular result happens. *If this is true, then this is an extraordinary promise.* Paul uses this phrase only one other time in Galatians 6, where he says that neither circumcision nor uncircumcision mean anything; what counts is a new creation. "New creation" is not a weak catchphrase. The words contain power and hope.

These thoughts return me to the promise. For anyone who is in Christ, there is a new creation. It does not say there *will* be or there *will* come. There *is* a new creation—already in existence. We don't have to make it; we get to notice, then add and modify it—within us and surrounding us.

What are we to notice? One of Paul's last points to the Corinthians is, "So we have stopped evaluating others from a human point of view" (2 Cor 5:16 NLT). Here, Paul declares that we will no longer look upon any other person from a human standpoint, just as he has learned to behold Christ himself as the incarnate God, not simply as newborn baby. For once we have discerned Jesus to be savior of the world, we cannot limit our estimate of other human beings—the born or unborn, exploiters or murderers, terrorists or militarists, frauds or failures—as dwelling beyond the reach of Love.

NOTES

1   Barbara Taylor Brown, "Learning to Wait in the Dark: A Holy Saturday Reflection," *Huffington Post*, last modified June 18, 2014, https://www.huffpost.com/entry/learning-to-wait-in-the-dark_b_5175191.

2   M Jade Kaiser, "Behold, this glistening of hope," poetic reflection from "A Contemplative Epiphany Service," Enfleshed, last modified March 8, 2023, https://enfleshed.com/liturgy/annual/. Used with permission.

3   Zora Neale Hurston, *Their Eyes Were Watching God* (New York: Harper Collins, 2006), 158.

4   Morgan Harper Nichols (@morganharpernichols), "There is a reason the sky gets dark at night," Instagram, May 6, 2019, https://www.instagram.com/p/BxH7s5YA_ED/.

5   Tamar Kadari, "Wife of Job: Midrash and Aggadah," *Shalvi/Hyman Encyclopedia of Jewish Women*, December 31, 1999, jwa.org/encyclopedia/article/wife-of-job-midrash-and-aggadah.

6   Audre Lorde, "Living with Cancer" and "Epilogue," in *A Burst of Light and Other Essays* (New York: Mineola, 2017), 53, 209. First published 1988. Used with permission.

7   Pádraig Ó Tuama, *In the Shelter: Finding a Home in the World* (London: Hodder and Stoughton, 2015), 20.

8   Quoted in Richard Rohr, *Breathing Under Water: Spirituality and the Twelve Steps* (Cincinnati: Franciscan Media, 2011), 38–39. For various translations of the Gospel of Thomas, see http://www.gnosis.org/naghamm/nhl_thomas.htm.

9   Cherríe Moraga, preface to *This Bridge Called My Back*, 4th ed., ed. Cherríe Moraga and Gloria Anzaldúa (Albany: State University of New York Press, 2015), xlx.

10 Howard Thurman, *Jesus and the Disinherited* (Boston: Beacon Press, 1996), 112.

11 Howard Thurman, "Christmas Is Waiting to Be Born," in *The Mood of Christmas and Other Celebrations* (Richmond: Friends United Press, 1985), 21. Used with permission.

12 Martin Luther King Jr., *The Radical King*, ed. Cornell West (Boston: Beacon, 2016), 169–70.

13 Toni Morrison, *Beloved* (New York: Vintage International, 2004), 102.

14 Cole Arthur Riley, *This Here Flesh: Spirituality, Liberation, and the Stories That Make Us* (New York: Convergent, 2022), 194. Excerpt(s) from THIS HERE FLESH: SPIRITUALITY, LIBERATION, AND THE STORIES THAT MAKE US by Cole Arthur Riley, copyright © 2022 by Cole Arthur Riley. Used by permission of Convergent Books, an imprint of Random House, a division of Penguin Random House LLC. All rights reserved.

15 Jan Richardson, "As on a Day of Festival," in *Circle of Grace: A Book of Blessings for the Seasons* (Orlando: Wanton Gospeller Press, 2015), 49–50. "As on a Day of Festival" Jan Richardson from *Circle of Grace: A Book of Blessings for the Seasons*. Used by permission. janrichardson.com.

16 Marlene Kropf, "God of Deep and Dazzling Darkness," in *Sing the Story* (Scottdale: Faith & Life Resources, 2007), #129. Used with permission.

17 Richard Rohr, "Being Called Again: A Second and Deeper Innocence," *Oneing: Innocence* 3, no. 2 (2017): 87.

18 Richard Rohr, *The Divine Dance: The Trinity and Your Transformation* (Whitaker House: 2016), 100.

19 *The CEB Women's Bible* (Nashville: Common English Bible, 2016), 607–8.

20 Center for Action and Contemplation, "Welcome Darkness and Mystery," *Daily Meditations*, July 19, 2017, https://cac.org/welcome-darkness-mystery-2017-07-19/.

21 David Wright, "Sing and sing," in *A Liturgy for Stones* (Telford: Cascadia, 2003). Used with permission.

22 George Dupuy, "To look on God's face," in *Sing the Story* (Scottdale: Faith & Life Resources, 2007), #133. Used with permission.

23 Iona Community, "From where we are," in *Stages on the Way: Worship Resources and Readings for Lent, Holy Week, and Easter* (Glasgow: Wild Goose Resource Group, 2000). Used with permission.

THE AUTHOR

SHANNON DYCUS is vice president of student affairs and dean of students at Eastern Mennonite University in Harrisonburg, Virginia, and author of the women's Bible study *Every Time I Feel the Spirit* with Herald Press. She was previously co-pastor at First Mennonite Church in Indianapolis, supporting the spiritual formation of that community through preaching and teaching. Shannon holds a degree in secondary education from Butler University and received her master of divinity from Christian Theological Seminary. With passion for holistically journeying with people, Shannon is also a trained spiritual director through San Francisco Theological Seminary. Shannon is active in writing and worship development roles with Mennonite Church USA.